Everything Romantic

A BOOK FOR LOVERS

Michael Newman

MJF BOOKS
NEW YORK

Published by MJF Books
Fine Communications
322 Eighth Avenue
New York, NY 10001

Everything Romantic
LC Control Number 2002114268
ISBN 1-56731-567-4

Copyright © 1995 by Michael Newman

This edition published in arrangement with Citadel Press, an imprint of
Kensington Publishing Corp.

Manufactured in the United States of America on acid-free paper ∞

MJF Books and the MJF colophon are trademarks of Fine Creative
Media, Inc.

QM   10   9   8   7   6   5   4   3   2   1

Contents

Preface   vii

Acknowledgments   ix

What Is Romance?   1

The True Romantic   4

Your Romantic I.Q.   7

The ABCs of Romance   10

Creative Celebrations   12

Inspired Anniversaries   27

Saying "I Love You"   30

Writing Love Letters   36

Sending Love Poetry   39

The Language of Flowers   46

The Gift of Music   57

How to Send Messages With Gems   61

Books of Love   68

The Big Picture   73

A Boy Named Sue   80

What's in a Name?   89

Romantic Gifts for Those on a Budget   112

Truly Romantic Gifts 116

Timely Trivia 120

The Gift of Time 136

Playful Aphrodisiacs 139

Erotica 143

Tantalizing Aromas 147

Sensual Seduction 152

An Enchanting Evening 156

Wine for Romantic Occasion 160

Love Potions 163

Heavenly Love 169

Beautiful Dreamer 178

Romantic Dates for Two 183

Romantic Dates Extraordinaire 186

Romantic Vacations 188

Exotic Vacations 191

The Ultimate Gift 197

Romantic Marriage Proposals 204

Wedding Omens and Customs 208

Wedding Vows 212

Romantic Honeymoons 220

Parting Notes 223

Preface

Romance is so very much more than gestures, kindnesses, and declarations of love and affection. It also is everything that goes to make up an *attitude*—a genuine desire to relate to the whole other person; to become, with heartfelt enthusiasm and joy, as one with your lover's needs and desires.

Romance begins with the awareness that the person you care so very much for responds to life and love very much as you do—with all five senses: *sight, smell, hearing, taste,* and *feel.* As a true romantic, you must find ways to fulfill all of these.

Everything Romantic: A Book for Lovers will help you to understand, feel, and visualize the significance of romance in a relationship. Unique and creative ideas in this book will activate your imagination and show you ways to both satisfy your sweetheart's senses and win his or her heart through learning to effectively express your love.

Acknowledgments

I would like to extend a special thank-you to my many friends who believed in the idea behind this book and were always there with words of encouragement and a willing-ness to listen. Special among them are Florence and Tom Emery, Steve Garcia, Don and Anna Gruhl, Ed and Kerrie Hanzel, Mary Pat Hennessy, Len Lanzi, Remy and Bernie Ordona, Joe Ortega, Renee and Mario Spiazzi, Don and Kaye Templeman, Bob and Elizabeth Vega, Dwayne and Marie Waltrip, and Tina Weber. I would also like to thank my editor, Denise O'Sullivan, whose abundant patience and hard work helped make this book a reality. Most important, I want to thank my wife, Peggy, and my daughters, Dawn and Michelle, for their priceless support and encouragement.

Everything Romantic

What Is Romance?

The word *romance* is wonderfully descriptive. It conjures up visions of a world long gone, though not quite forgotten. A world in which chivalry, courtship, manners, and love were an important part of life. An age when passion, inspiration, zeal, and enthusiasm often seemed all that mattered. Indeed, *romance* evokes memories of the days when love meant virtually everything. Think of Sir Lancelot and Lady Guinevere and the absolute love they shared. And back to Julius Caesar and Cleopatra, and the empires their consuming love created and almost destroyed.

Cynics say that romance no longer exists—that it is a figment of our collective imagination derived from ancient legends and so-called old wives' tales that don't fit today's lifestyles. And that it is foolish and juvenile behavior and an utter waste of time. Given our need for two-earner incomes, they say, with the attendant toll of job-related societal stress, and heavy demands on the family, there is no time for romance. No time for love. Those just aren't practical anymore.

However, ask these cynics if they have a romantic memory and you will usually find that they do (even if it takes some prodding to get it out). And that memory, that absolutely wonderful memory, coupled with their marvelous human imagination, brings back to them extraordinary feelings that would melt even the hardest of hearts.

The Essence of Romance

The essence of romance is giving of yourself continually, without reservation or condition but with joy and absolute enthusiasm. It is just that sort of giving that makes it romance. Without giving, it is technique—nothing more.

Romance gives a relationship grace and meaning. It is an expression of genuine love and affection. To be romantic, you must be generous with your concern, caring, and affection. This requires sensitivity and doing well-planned things that show you care.

Romance entails a degree of formality and restraint, an acknowledgment that your enamorata's feelings and desires really matter to you, and a yearning to fulfill the whims and needs of his or her soul by being considerate, caring, and loving.

Romantic Courtships

The word *courtship* comes from the royal courts of old wherein calls for decent behavior were paramount and courtship involved caring concern, kindness, and imagination. Even today (especially today), successful courtships that are fulfilling to both lovers rely heavily on romance. This is the key to keeping love alive and vibrant.

But romance is more than just courtship: No matter what else you do in your relationship—no matter how often you send flowers, write love letters or poems, or prepare candlelight dinners—you must always love your loved one in the ways he or she wants to be loved. Find out what these are and indulge them lavishly.

To do this you must learn to understand your beloved's aspirations, fantasies, pleasures. Therefore:

♥ Let him or her express thoughts openly and freely, without fear of ridicule.

♥ Show a real interest in his or her friends, activities, and interests and notice the things they wear and do—and compliment them on those frequently.

♥ Share your thoughts and feelings in order to create an atmosphere of trust, intimacy, and understanding.

♥ Show an interest in his or her goals and support the achievement thereof.

♥ Remember special occasions.

The Art of Romance

To be effective, romance must be an ongoing and constant love affair. Without continual loving care, romance—like a rose—will wither and die. And with it will go the ambience that initially enabled it to grow so beautifully. Put another way, the art of romance is a moment-to-moment way of life. It begins with caring and imagination, glides into creativity and fantasy, and progresses to mutual concern and ecstasy—becoming more and more meaningful to the couple in love.

"The Romantic's Bill of Rights" states: "It is the inalienable right of every true romantic to practice wise time management; plan activities in advance; have a mature outlook on life and relationships; be generous, open to new ideas, and willing to make a commitment (and be creative in that commitment); be empathetic and patient; refrain from being jealous; be attentive; work at being a good role model; be interesting; and know oneself..."

The True Romantic

As you embark on your enchant-
ing journey of romantic pursuit, it is important to keep in mind that the
true romantic:

♥ Takes romance seriously and spends the time "doing it right"

♥ Is always considerate, loving, and kind in gestures toward and treatment of the one loved, and supportive of the loved one's activities,
   friendships, and needs

♥ Gives without expectations and without ulterior motives

♥ Is spontaneous and will forever find ways to surprise a loved one

♥ Is flexible and adaptable, willing to participate in spur-of-the-moment
   activities that bring that special someone happiness and joy

♥ Works at being a mind reader

♥ Finds ways to be more interesting to the loved one by constantly learning to do things they both can enjoy and benefit from (e.g., cooking or
   playing a musical instrument)

   True romantics actively live by the "Gospel of Romance," knowing that without this knowledge everything they do for their loved one is a gesture of something they want the other to have rather than a gift of something their loved one really wants or will get excited about. Simply put, a true romantic seeks to satisfy a loved one's deepest wants, desires, and aspirations through true caring and understanding.

How many questions about your loved one do you know the answers to?

1. What is the color of her/his eyes?

2. What is the color of her/his hair?

3. What is her/his favorite color?

4. Is he/she a winter, spring, summer, or fall color fan?

5. What size skirt, dress, blouse, jeans, shoes, etc., does she wear? What size shirt, pants, jacket, shoes, etc., does he wear?

6. What is her/his favorite style of clothes? Does he/she have a favorite designer?

7. Does he/she enjoy wearing jewelry? What is his/her favorite style?

8. Does she like to wear a scarf? What kind of tie does he like to wear?

9. What is her favorite perfume? What is his favorite aftershave/cologne?

10. Does he/she like to read? What is her/his favorite subject matter? Does he/she have a preferred author? Does he/she enjoy reading poetry?

11. What kind of music does he/she enjoy most? Which artists bring her/him the most pleasure?

12. Does he/she like to dance?

13. Does he/she enjoy going to comedy workshops? Plays? The symphony? Modern concerts? (Which artists?)

14. What is her/his favorite movie of all time?

15. Who is her/his favorite actress? Actor?

16. Does he/she believe in role models? Who is her/his "hero"?

17. What is her/his favorite flower? Why?

18. What is her/his favorite dessert? Snack? Entree?

19. Does he/she enjoy wine? Which does he/she prefer?

20. What is her/his favorite time of year? Why?

21. What is her/his favorite time of day for…?

22. What does he/she enjoy doing most? Does he/she have a favorite hobby, activity, or sport? Does he/she prefer the mountains, the desert, the beach—or someplace else?

23. Does he/she collect anything? What are the special needs he/she attaches to her/his collection?

24. Does he/she like animals? Which ones?

25. If he/she could go anywhere in this world with you, where would it be?

26. If he/she could do anything, be anyone, have anything—what would he/she want to do, be, or have?

   By knowing these answers and making this knowledge part of your consciousness and daily routine, romance will flourish in your life!

"The Gospel of Romance" is by far the most important rule a romantic can live by. It states: "Thou shalt know thy love and thy love's special needs—completely, absolutely, passionately."

Your Romantic I.Q.

It has been said that every journey begins with a single step. But that first small step can actually be a giant leap of faith, because it is in effect simultaneously the realization and self-affirmation of where you are starting from and what your ultimate destination is going to be. The journey to becoming a true romantic is no different. You must first understand where you are starting from to know how far you must go, and realize and accept what you must learn and do in order to reach your desired goal.

The following self-evaluation quiz should help you find where you are in being a true romantic. Select the answers (one per question) that best describe you. You can total your score by referring to the answers at the end of the chapter.

1. I show my affection for my loved one by:
    a. telling him/her "I love you" at least once a week
    b. sending periodic love notes or letters
    c. constant daily reminders and loving gestures
    d. N/A (He or she should know of my love.)

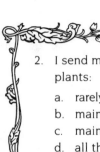

2. I send my loved one flowers, balloons, and/or plants:

   a. rarely if ever because it's a waste of money
   b. mainly on Valentine's Day
   c. mainly on Mother's Day
   d. all the time (I don't need a reason)

3. My idea of a romantic getaway is:

   a. making spur-of-the-moment transportation and lodging reservations and taking an unplanned trip for two to a romantic paradise like the Fiji Islands or Acapulco
   b. checking into a bed-and-breakfast for the weekend so the two of us can be alone, away from the outside world
   c. taking a well-planned trip to a romantic city like San Francisco, New Orleans, or New York
   d. taking a trip with friends or family

4. I am at my romantic best when I am

   a. telling sexy, off-color jokes
   b. passionate and attentive
   c. sensitive, compassionate, and caring
   d. acting like a perfect gentleman or lady

5. I like my loved one to be

   a. physically attractive to strangers
   b. kind, understanding, and caring
   c. interesting, faithful, and daring
   d. interested only in me and my interests

6. My favorite holiday is:

   a. the anniversary of the day I met my loved one

   b. Independence Day
   c. New Year's Eve
   d. Valentine's Day

7. My loved one appreciates me most when I

   a. repeatedly say how much I love her/him
   b. show a genuine interest, give heartfelt compliments, and show my love in a variety of loving ways
   c. offer constructive criticism to make her/him a better person
   d. remember his/her birthday and Valentine's Day (especially considering how busy I am)

8. When I select a gift for my loved one, it is

   a. something I like that I really want her/him to have
   b. something we saw together and he/she seemed to be interested in
   c. a choice I make based on her/his interests, desires, and needs—not on my own
   d. something based on a suggestion of a sales clerk

9. If my loved one were asked to appear as a guest on a national talk show whose topic was "Is Romance Still Alive?" I would

   a. convince her/him not to appear on the show
   b. invite everyone I know to watch the program with me
   c. tell everybody I know about the show
   d. wonder what he/she was going to say

10. On a romantic scale of 1 to 10 (10 being the best), my loved one would rate me:

a. 8-10   b. 5-7   c. 2-4   d. 0-1

If you scored between 98 and 100, congratulations! You _are_ a true romantic with a life full of love, happiness, and passionate adventure ahead of you!

If you scored between 91 and 97, you are one of the most romantic people anywhere, and well on your way to _becoming_ a true romantic.

If you scored between 70 and 90, you still show promise. Reading this entire book will help raise your score appreciably.

If you scored between 50 and 69, lock yourself in your room until you have both read and mastered this book—no matter how long it takes!

If you scored between 3 and 49, you need to ask yourself "Do I really want to be a true romantic?" and let your answer be your guide to what you do next. Romance can be a wonderful way of life, but it has to be the way you _want_ in order for it to enhance your relationship with your loved one.

Finally, if you scored between 0 and 2— well, romance may not be your forte. But there is hope. Use this book to reach your romantic potential!

Question Number	Quiz Answer: a.	b.	c.	d.	Your Score
1	3	7	10	0	_____
2	0	7	3	10	_____
3	10	7	3	0	_____
4	0	10	7	3	_____
5	0	7	10	0	_____
6	10	0	3	7	_____
7	7	10	0	3	_____
8	3	7	10	0	_____
9	0	10	7	3	_____
10	10	7	3	0	_____
Total Score					_____

Bon voyage, mon ami!

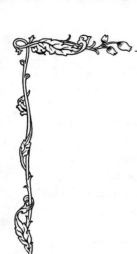

The ABCs of Romance

A true romantic knows that for love to last it needs to be cultivated and nurtured and that romance is the key to a successful loving relationship.

A true romantic is *attentive* to the beloved's needs and desires. He or she *cherishes* the time spent with the loved one, letting the sweetheart know how desirable he/she is.

True romantics experience *ecstasy* in their loving relationship and are *faithful* in their intentions and *generous* with their love. They find *happiness* in everything they do with the loved one, enjoying the *intimacy* that comes from loving that special person.

A true romantic derives *joy* from the pleasure of being with the loved one, looks forward to that next *kiss* and the *lovemaking* that inevitably follows, and relishes the *monogomous* relationship. She or he *nurtures* the sweetheart by providing an emotional *oasis* for her/him to come to when in need of comfort, support, and reassurance, knowing how *precious* of a gift that love is and how important the *quality* of that love can be.

A true romantic believes in the importance of *romance*, regularly showering the loved one with *spontaneous* and *thoughtful* gifts and compliments. She or he also seeks to be *understood* by her/his lover at all times.

The true romantic *values* the time spent with the loved one and *wants* to please him/her whenever possible. She or he strives to make life with the sweetheart into a special *Xanadu* for two, *yearning* to fulfill the loved one's needs with the *zeal* with which Romeo pursued Juliet and Cleopatra loved Caesar.

"Romance has been elegantly defined as the offspring of fiction and love."
—Disraeli

Creative
Celebrations

 true romantic seeks out occasions and works at making them special for the loved one. Some occasions are of course "required," by societal and federal pressure, but the best celebrations are the ones you make up on your own.

Required occasions include birthdays, your mutual anniversary of partnership, St. Valentine's Day (February 14), Mother's Day (second Sunday in May), Memorial Day (last Monday in May), Independence Day (July 4), Labor Day (first Monday in September), Veterans Day (November 11), Thanksgiving (fourth Thursday in November), Hanukkah (November or December), Christmas (December 25), New Year's Eve (December 31), and New Year's Day (January 1).

You also have a number of religious holidays to consider (a few of which have just been cited as required occasions): Epiphany, Ramadhan, Laitat Al-Qadr, Id Al-Fitr, Ash Wednesday, Purim, Palm Sunday, Passover, Good Friday, Easter, Ascension Day, Shavuot, Assumption, Rosh Hashanah, Yom Kippur, All Saints' Day, Advent, Hanukkah, and Christmas—to name several. Government holidays include Martin Luther King, Jr.'s Birthday, Inauguration Day, Lincoln's Birthday, Washington's Birthday (celebrated as President's Day to include Lincoln's Birthday), Loyalty Day, Armed Forces

Day, Memorial Day, Flag Day, Independence Day, Labor Day, Citizenship Day, Columbus Day, Election Day, Veterans Day, and Pearl Harbor Day.

Then there are the so-called fun occasions true romantics live for! The moments that they can plan unexpected, delightful activities around. The times when fantasy and reality can be combined into a blend of chemistry that explodes into a wonder of passion and love.

"Fun" occasions include nights during which there is a full moon; the beginning of spring, summer, fall, or winter; the first day it snows; the first flower that blooms; any kind of good news (and, similarly, the fact you didn't receive any bad news). Too, you might try creating special anniversaries (i.e., daily, monthly, quarterly, six-month, or standard annual ones) to suit almost any occasion whose memory is important to your loved one (when you met, when you went on your first date, when you got engaged, the first time you…)—as well as to you.

Here are some suggestions for starters—but you really should make up your own list. With the right memos at hand and the right attitude in mind, any and every day can become a special occasion for you and yours!

Day/Dated	**Special Occasions**
January 1	New Year's Day, Paul Revere's birthday, and Bonza Bottler Day (held on 1/1, 2/2, 3/3, 4/4, 5/5, 6/6, 7/7, 8/8, 9/9, 10/10, 11/11 & 12/12)
January 2	Anniversary of the first spacecraft orbit of the Sun
January 3	Tom Sawyer's cat's birthday
January 4	Trivia Day
January 5	"Thank Goodness We've Had Five Whole Days Without a Single Party That We _Had_ to Go to" Day
January 6	Armenian Christmas
January 7	Anniversary of the first balloon flight across the English Channel
January 8	National Joygerm Day
January 9	Show-and-Tell Day at Work
January 10	Anniversary of the League of Nations, and Man-Watchers' Week
January 11	Cuckoo Dancing Week (honors Laurel and Hardy, whose theme was "The Dancing Cuckoo")

January 12	Birthday of HAL (the 2001 computer)
January 13	Anniversary of first public broadcast of radio in New York, 1910
Second Wednesday	Make Your Dreams Come True Day
January 14	Anniversary of docking in space by *Soyuz* 4 and *Soyuz* 5
January 15	Humanitarian Day
Third Wednesday	Maintenance Day
Third Friday	Hat Day
January 16	National Nothing Day
Third Saturday	International Hot-and-Spicy Food Day
January 17	Benjamin Franklin's birthday
January 18	Human Relations Day, and Pooh Day
January 19	National Printing Ink Day
January 20	Inauguration Day
January 21	National Hugging Day
January 22	"Answer Your Cat's Question" Day
January 23	National Pie Day
January 24	Anniversary of the discovery of gold in California
January 25	Anniversary of the first Emmy Awards presentation
January 26	Australia Day (Australia)
January 27	Wolfgang Amadeus Mozart's birthday, and Thomas Crapper Day
January 28	National Kazoo Day
January 29	Backwards Day
January 30	Anniversary of the Beatles' last appearance together
January 31	Franz Schubert's birthday and anniversary of the crowning of the first Miss Albania
Superbowl Sunday	National Popcorn Day
February 1	Creative Romance Month, Human Relations Month, and Great American Pies Month
February 2	Groundhog Day
February 3	Halfway point of Winter
February 4	Torture Abolition Day
February 5	Weatherman's Day

February 6	Midwinter's Day
February 7	Ballet introduced in the United States
February 8	First opera performed in the United States
February 9	Gypsy Rose Lee's birthday
February 10	"All the News That's Fit to Print" Day
February 11	White Shirt Day, and the anniversary of Jack Paar's "Water Closet Incident"
February 12	Safetypup's birthday
February 13	Get a Different Name Day
February 14	St. Valentine's Day, and Skeezix Wallet's birthday
February 15	Lupercalia Fertility Festival
February 16	Independence Day (Lithuania)
February 17	National PTA Founder's Day
February 18	Anniversaries of the discovery of the planet Pluto and of the first cow to be milked while flying in an airplane
February 19	Anniversaries of the patenting of the phonograph and of the awarding of the first Bollingen Prize for Poetry
February 20	Student Volunteer Day
February 21	Birthday of _The New Yorker_
February 22	Anniversary of popcorn being introduced to the (wary) colonists
February 23	George Frideric Handel's birthday
February 24	Independence Day (Estonia)
February 25	Pierre Auguste Renoir's birthday
February 26	Buffalo Bill's birthday
February 27	Independence Day (Dominican Republic)
February 28	Anniversary of the final episode of M*A*S*H
February 29	Leap Year Day
March 1	Poetry Month and National Women's History Month
March 2	Texas Independence Day
March 3	"I Want You to Be Happy" Day
March 4	Anniversary of the formation of the Television Academy Hall of Fame
March 5	Hemlock Day

March 6	Michelangelo's birthday
March 7	Jane L. Slight's birthday
March 8	International [Working] Women's Day
March 9	Panic Day
March 10	Anniversary of the invention of the telephone
March 11	Rev. Edwin McGee's birthday, and Johnny Appleseed Day
March 12	Anniversary of Franklin D. Roosevelt's first "Fireside Chat"
March 13	Good Samaritan Involvement Day
March 14	Plant a Flower Day & Mothers Day (a day set aside to honor moth collectors)
March 15	Buzzards' Day
March 16	Goddard Day (On this day in 1926, Robert Hutchings Goddard launched the world's first liquid-propellant rocket)
March 17	St. Patrick's Day
March 18	Anniversary of the first electric razor, by Schick, Inc., in 1931
March 19	Swallows return to San Juan Capistrano
March 20	Forever True to You Day
March 21	Fragrance Day, and Johann Sebastian Bach's birthday
March 22	National Goof-Off Day
March 23	Near-Miss Day
March 24	St. Gabriel Feast Day
March 25	Global Understanding Day
March 26	"Make Up Your Own Holiday" Day
March 27	National Joe/Joanna Day
March 28	Teachers Day (Czechoslovakia)
March 29	Knights of Columbus Founder's Day
March 30	Van Gogh's birthday
March 31	Anniversary of the completion of the Eiffel Tower
April 1	April Fool's Day
April 2	Giovanni Giacomo Casanova's birthday
April 3	Celebrate Woman Day, and "Sorry Charlie" [the Tuna] Day
April 4	Anniversary of the election of the first woman mayor in the United States

April 5	Chicken Little Awards Day
April 6	North Pole discovered
April 7	World Health Day
April 8	Flower Festival (Japan)
April 9	Winston Churchill Day
April 10	Commodore Perry Day
April 11	Barbershop Quartet Day
April 12	Big Wind Day
April 13	Thomas Jefferson's birthday
April 14	Pan-American Day
April 15	Rubber Eraser Day, the anniversary of the sinking of the Titanic, and Income Tax Day
April 16	National Stress Awareness Day
April 17	Verrazano Day (commemorating the discovery of New York Harbor)
April 18	Anniversary of Paul Revere's ride
April 19	John Parker Day
April 20	Library Legislative Day
April 21	Birthday of Rome
Third Thursday	Look-Alike Day
April 22	International Special Librarians Day
April 23	Lovers Day (Spain), and Read Me Day
April 24	Anniversary of the establishment of the Library of Congress (1800)
April 25	Anniversary of the Hubble telescope's deployment in space
April 26	Hug an Australian Day
April 27	Independence Day (Sierra Leone and Togo)
April 28	Great Poetry Reading Day, and Kiss-Your-Mate Day
April 29	Greenery Day (Japan)
April 30	National Honesty Day
May 1	May Day, the anniversary of the opening of the Empire State Building, and Lei Day
May 2	National Homebrew Day
May 3	Lumpy Rug Day

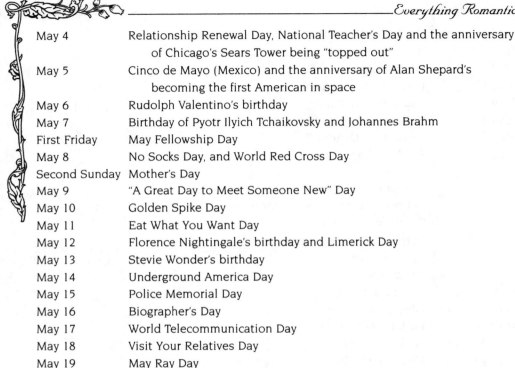

May 4	Relationship Renewal Day, National Teacher's Day and the anniversary of Chicago's Sears Tower being "topped out"
May 5	Cinco de Mayo (Mexico) and the anniversary of Alan Shepard's becoming the first American in space
May 6	Rudolph Valentino's birthday
May 7	Birthday of Pyotr Ilyich Tchaikovsky and Johannes Brahm
First Friday	May Fellowship Day
May 8	No Socks Day, and World Red Cross Day
Second Sunday	Mother's Day
May 9	"A Great Day to Meet Someone New" Day
May 10	Golden Spike Day
May 11	Eat What You Want Day
May 12	Florence Nightingale's birthday and Limerick Day
May 13	Stevie Wonder's birthday
May 14	Underground America Day
May 15	Police Memorial Day
May 16	Biographer's Day
May 17	World Telecommunication Day
May 18	Visit Your Relatives Day
May 19	May Ray Day
May 20	Eliza Doolittle Day
May 21	Red Cross founded
May 22	Anniversary of "There Goes Johnny" Night
May 23	Linnaeus Day (Sweden)
May 24	Anniversary of the opening of the Brooklyn Bridge
May 25	National Tap Dance Day
May 26	Feast of St. Augustine of Canterbury
May 27	Anniversary of RMS Queen *Mary*'s maiden voyage
May 28	St. Bernard of Montjoux Feast Day
May 29	Anniversary of the first time Mt. Everest was scaled, and of Bing Crosby's recording of "White Christmas"
May 30	Memorial Day and anniversary of the publication of the first American

	daily newspaper
May 31	Weeding of the Sea Feast (Italy)
June 1	National Rose Month
June 2	Yell "Fudge" at the Cobras in North America Day
June 3	Anniversary of Mighty Casey's striking out
June 4	Anniversary of the awarding of the first Pulitzer Prize
First Friday and Saturday	Donut Day
June 5	World Environment Day
June 6	National Yo-Yo Day
June 7	Boone Day
June 8	Anniversary of the proposal of the Bill of Rights
June 9	Donald Duck's birthday
June 10	Joyful Summer Celebration Day
June 11	King Kamehameha I Day
June 12	Anniversary of the founding of the National Baseball Hall of Fame
Second Sunday	Children's Day
June 13	Race Unity Day
June 14	Birthday of Univac (the computer)
June 15	National Hug Day, and Magna Carta Day
June 16	Jefferson Awards ceremony
June 17	Watergate Day
June 18	Anniversary of the first time an American woman who participated in a space flight
June 19	Garfield the Cat's Birthday
June 20	Anniversary of the first honeymoon in a balloon gondola
June 21	Summer Solstice
June 22	National Columnists Day
June 23	Discovery Day (Newfoundland)
June 24	Anniversary of the first sighting of a UFO
June 25	Anniversary of the first color TV broadcast, and of Peggy Ann Newman's birthday
June 26	Independence Day (Madagascar)

June 27	"Happy Birthday To You" Day
June 28	Anniversary of the Monday Holiday Law
June 29	Peter and Paul Day
June 30	The anniversary of Blondin's crossing of Niagara Falls on a tightrope, and Leap Second Adjustment Day
July 1	Pleasure Week begins, and the anniversary of the introduction of color TV
July 2	Anniversary of the Civil Rights Act of 1964
July 3	Compliment Your Mirror Day (for having such a wonderful owner)
July 4	Independence Day
July 5	Man-watcher's Compliment Week
July 6	Anniversary of the appointment of the first black United States Attorney
July 7	Star Festival (Japan)
July 8	Video Games Day
July 9	Anniversary of the ratification of the Fourteenth Amendment
July 10	Clerihew Day
July 11	Special Recreation Day
July 12	Henry David Thoreau's and Michelle Lynn Newman's birthday
July 13	Anniversary of the "Live Aid" Concerts
July 14	Bastille Day (France)
July 15	Respect Canada Day
July 16	Apollo spacecraft launched
July 17	"Wrong Way" Corrigan Day
July 18	National Ice Cream Day, and the anniversary of the opening of Disneyland
July 19	Anniversary of the first Women's Convention
July 20	Moon Day, and Anniversary of the signing of the Geneva Accords
July 21	Anniversary of the dedication of the National Women's Hall of Fame
July 22	Rat-Catcher's Day and Spooners Day
July 23	Make a Big Splash Day!
July 24	Pioneer Day (Utah)
July 25	Cave Man Never Day
Last Sunday	Comedy Celebration Day
July 26	New York Ratification Day

July 27	Anniversary of the successful completion of the Atlantic Telegraph Cable
July 28	Anniversary of the first singing telegram
July 29	Anniversary of the founding of NASA
July 30	Independence Day (Vanuatu)
July 31	Anniversary of the first federal patent
First Sunday	Friendship Day, American Family Day, and Celebration of Peace Day
August 1	Romance Awareness Month
August 2	Anniversary of the *actual* signing of the Declaration of Independence
August 3	Anniversary of Christopher Columbus's original departure from Spain
August 4	Raoul Wallenberg's birthday
August 5	Anniversary of the founding of the first colony in North America
August 6	Independence Day (Bolivia)
August 7	Halfway point of Summer
August 8	Odie's birthday
First Monday	National Smile Week
Second Sunday	Family Day
August 9	Independence Day (Singapore)
August 10	Independence Day (Ecuador)
August 11	Presidential Joke Day
August 12	Jersey Battle of Flowers Day (England)
August 13	International Lefthandedness Day
First Friday the Thirteenth	Blame Someone Else Day
August 14	Liberty Tree Day, and Middle Children Day
August 15	National Relaxation Day
August 16	Joe Miller's Joke Day
August 17	Anniversary of the first balloon crossing of the Atlantic
August 18	Anniversary of the ratification of the Nineteenth Amendment
August 19	National Aviation Day
August 20	Anniversary of the launching of Voyager 2
August 21	Anniversary of Hawaii's becoming our 50th state, and Ozma's (the Queen of Oz's) birthday
August 22	Anniversary of *America* winning the America's Cup and bringing it to

	the New York Yacht Club
August 23	Anniversary of the first man-powered flight
August 24	Vesuvius Day (Italy)
August 25	Kiss-and-Make-Up Day
August 26	Women's Equality Day
August 27	Mother Teresa's birthday, and The Duchess Who Wasn't Day
August 28	Dream Day
August 29	According To Hoyle Day
August 30	Huey P. Long Day (and my anniversary!)
August 31	Independence Day (Trinidad & Tobago)
September 1	National Courtesy Month, National Honey Month and Self-Improvement Month
September 2	Bison-Ten-Yell Day
September 3	Anniversary of the beginning of the Penny Press
September 4	Newspaper Career Day
September 5	"Be Late for Something" Day
September 6	Anniversary of the completion of the first nonstop marine circumnavigation
September 7	"Neither Snow Nor Rain" Day
September 8	World Literacy Day
September 9	Admission Day (California)
September 10	Swap Ideas Day
September 11	"No News Is Good News" Day
September 12	National Grandparents Day
September 13	Annual "Fearless Forecasts of TV's Fall Flops" made
September 14	Anniversary of the first successful solo transatlantic balloon crossing
September 15	Anniversary of the world record for most kisses, set by Alfred A. E. Wolfram of New Brighton, Minn., who kissed 8,001 people in eight hours at the Minnesota Rennaissance Festival in 1990
September 16	Mayflower Day
September 17	Citizenship Day
September 18	Independence Day (Chile)

September 19	Saint Januarius (Gennaro) Feast Day
September 20	Anniversary of the tennis "Battle of the Sexes," won by Billie Jean King
September 21	World Gratitude Day
September 22	Anniversary of the first ice cream cone, Proposal Day, and Hobbit Day
September 23	Checkers Day
September 24	National Laundry Workers Day
September 25	Everybody's Day
September 26	National Good Neighbor Day, and "The Best Day of My Life" Day
September 27	Ancestor Appreciation Day
September 28	Cabrillo Day
September 29	Goose Day
September 30	Independence Day (Botswana)
October 1	National Dessert Month, National Pizza Month, anniversary of the first World Series, and of the opening of Disney World
October 2	Charlie Brown's and Snoopy's birthday
October 3	Anniversary of the first broadcast of "The Andy Griffith Show"
October 4	World Habitat Day, and Ten-Four Day
October 5	Republic Day (Portugal)
October 6	Physician's Assistant Day
October 7	Archbishop Desmond Tutu's birthday
October 8	Anniversary of the Great Fire of Chicago
October 9	Leif Eriksson Day (Minnesota)
October 10	Health and Sports Day (Japan)
October 11	Thanksgiving (Canada)
October 12	Anniversary of Columbus's arrival in the Americas, and International Moment of Frustration Scream Day
October 13	Anniversary of the creation of the National Commission on Space
October 14	Anniversary of awarding of the Nobel Peace Prize to Martin Luther King, and Be Bald and Be Free Day
Third Saturday	Sweetest Day
October 15	National Grouch Day
October 16	Dictionary Day, and World Food Day

October 17	African-American Poetry Day
October 18	Alaska Day
October 19	"Evaluate Your Life" Day, and Anniversary Day
October 20	Kenyatta Day (Kenya)
October 21	Anniversary of the demonstration of the first incandescent light bulb
October 22	World's End Day
October 23	National Mole Day
October 24	United Nation's Day
Fourth Sunday	Mother-in-Law Day
October 25	Sourest Day
October 26	Horseless Carriage Day
October 27	Anniversary of the publication of the *Federalist* "papers"
October 28	Anniversary of Statue of Liberty Dedication
October 29	Founding Day (Turkey)
October 30	Devil's Night
October 31	Halloween
November 1	National Authors Day, and Recreation Day (Australia)
November 2	Election Day
November 3	Sandwich Day
November 4	Mischief Night (commemorating the failure of a plot to blow up the British houses of parliament in 1605)
November 5	World Community Day
November 6	Saxophone Day
First Saturday	Sadie Hawkins Day
November 7	Hug-a-Bear Day
November 8	Anniversary of the discovery of the X ray
November 9	Anniversary of the "fall" of the Berlin Wall
November 10	Anniversary of the first patent issued for windshield wipers
November 11	Anniversary of the first performance of "God Bless America"
November 12	Auguste Rodin's birthday
November 13	National Moms and Dads Day
November 14	Anniversary of the first successful blood transfusion

November 15 — American Enterprise Day

November 16 — Anniversary of the Skylab SL-4 launch, and Admission Day (Oklahoma)

November 17 — Homemade Bread Day

November 18 — Mickey Mouse's birthday

November 19 — Anniversary of Lincoln's Gettysburg Address, and "Have a Bad Day" Day

Friday before Thanksgiving — Doublespeak Awards Day

November 20 — Anniversary of the first state's ratification of the Bill of Rights

November 21 — World Hello Day

November 22 — Anniversary of the adoption of SOS as the international distress signal, and World "Stop the Violence" Day

November 23 — Anniversary of the first episode of "Dr. Who"

November 24 — Anniversary of the "D.B. Cooper" hijacking

November 25 — Shopping Reminder Day

November 26 — Anniversary of the first U.S. holiday created by presidential proclamation

Fourth Thursday — Thanksgiving

November 27 — New Year celebration (Hmong)

November 28 — Anniversary of opening of the Gershwin Theater (formerly the Uris Theater) on Broadway

November 29 — Louisa May Alcott's birthday

November 30 — "Stay Home Because You're Well" Day

December 1 — Universal Human Rights Month begins

December 2 — Anniversary of the day when AT&T handled a record 157.8 million calls, and Pan- American Health Day

First Thursday — Lover's Fair (Belgium)

December 3 — Admission Day (Illinois)

December 4 — Day of the Artisan

December 5 — Anniversary of the Repeal of Prohibition

December 6 — Anniversary of the ratification of the Thirteenth Amendment

December 7 — Anniversary of the first state's ratification of the Constitution (Delaware)

December 8 — Anniversary of the dissolution of the Soviet Union

December 9 — Independence Day (Tanzania)

December 10	Human Rights Day, and the anniversary of the awarding of the first Nobel Peace Prize
December 11	Anniversary of the establishment of UNICEF
December 12	Poinsettia Day
December 13	Annual naming of the Most Boring Celebrities of the Year
December 14	Anniversary of the arrival of the first explorers to reach the South Pole, and Admission Day (Alabama)
December 15	Anniversary of the ratification of the Bill of Rights
December 16	Ludwig van Beethoven's birthday
December 17	Underdog Day, and Pan-American Aviation Day
December 18	Anniversary of first performance of *The Nutcracker*
December 19	Anniversary of the first radio broadcast from space
December 20	Louisiana Purchase Day
December 21	Humbug Day, and the anniversary of the Pilgrims' landing at Plymouth Rock
December 22	The eve of the eve of Christmas Eve (also known as "Panic Day" for last-minute Christmas shoppers)
December 23	Anniversary of the first circumnavigational flight without refueling, by the *Voyager* (Dec. 14–23, 1986)
December 24	Christmas Eve
December 25	Christmas
December 26	Christmas (Germany), God-Awful Tie Day and Steve Allen's birthday
December 27	Anniversary of the Radio City Music Hall's opening
December 28	Anniversary of the first advertisement for *Poor Richards Almanack*
December 29	The admittance of Texas as twenty-eighth state in the Union
December 30	Rudyard Kipling's birthday
December 31	New Year's Eve, "Make Up Your Mind" Day, and "You're All Done" Day

As you can see, every day can be a holiday!

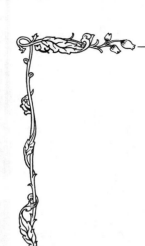

Inspired Anniversaries

If you really are a true romantic, you'll find yourself making up special remembrances—such as the fifth anniversary (day, week, fortnight, month, etc.) of the last time you watched the sun rise together; the second anniversary (hour, day, etc.) of the last time you made love; the umpteenth anniversary of the first day you met, your first date, your first kiss, the first time you said "I love you" to each other—you get the picture. And you'll plan unusually creative, thoughtful ways to celebrate them.

However, there is still the matter of the "official anniversary." So (since picking an anniversary gift isn't always easy) here are some suggestions you might consider:

Anniversary	Traditional	Modern	The Complete Guide's Pick
1	Paper	Clocks	Engraved champagne glasses
2	Cotton	China	Lingerie (works for both!)
3	Leather	Crystal	Dancing lessons for two
4	Silk/flowers	Appliances	Cooking lessons for two
5	Wood	Silverware	A romantic trip for two
6	Candy/iron	Wood	An 18" x 24" photograph of the two of you

Anniversary	Traditional	Modern	The Complete Guide's Pick
7	Wool/copper	Desk sets	Two dozen roses (the thorns help "scratch" the seven-year "itch"')
8	Bronze/rubber	Linens	A poem you wrote, calligraphed on parchment
9	Pottery	Leather	A day at a European spa being pampered, followed by dinner for two at an intimate restaurant
10	Tin	Diamond jewelry	Season tickets for two to (sure-bet choice of ballet, symphony, ball game, rock concert, etc.)
11	Steel	Fashion jewelry	A trip for two to San Francisco (complete with a tour of the wine country)
12	Linen	Pearls	A trip for two to Disney World
13	Lace	Textiles	A vacation for two in a mountain resort (complete with a gift of lingerie)
14	Ivory	Gold jewelry	A love song written and recorded just for your loved one (by you)
15	Crystal	Watches	Tickets for two to a play on Broadway (complete with accommodations and dinner)
20	China	Platinum	Week-long cruise for two
25	Silver	Silver	Silver*
30	Pearl	Pearl	Pearl*
35	Coral	Jade	Jade*
40	Ruby	Ruby	Ruby*
45	Sapphire	Sapphire	Sapphire*
50	Gold	Gold	Gold*
55	Emerald	Emerald	Emerald*
60	Diamond	Diamond	Diamond*

* These gifts require that careful, *imaginative* thought be given as to how you are going to present them—such as an emerald given on a cruise, a pearl "discovered" (perhaps in an oyster shell) while vacationing on a tropical island and given on a moonlit night;

a bracelet of rubies presented under a covered dish at the finest restaurant in Paris. Or, for something closer to home, how about presenting the gift at the top of a mountain, or by the edge of a waterfall, or over a "just-opened" pizza box? The gift doesn't have to be expensive to be meaningful!

As long as you put a little imagination into your gift, keeping in mind your loved one's special needs and desires, he or she will become—and remain—convinced that you are the most romantic, most thoughtful person of all time.

Saying "I Love You"

rue romantics are constantly looking for new ways to tell their loved ones "I Love You"—ways that show how much they care and how special their sweethearts are to them. And they just as constantly discover caring, daily "reminders" that say it all.

Sometimes this might be by means of a note taped to the toothpaste. Or on the refrigerator door. Or even on the computer. Other times it might be in the form of a small sign somewhere along a familiar stretch of road. Or on a billboard, for others to see. Or even as a message in the sky, visible for miles around.

It could be a letter composed of descriptions of memories you have shared—short phrases describing wonderful recollections that remind you of how much you love each other—and what your loved one means to you, your life, your very existence. You could even tell your sweetheart, in a different language nearly every day for a year, of your love for her or him. And that's where this book can help you directly—*right now*!

Not counting sign language (for which, see a dictionary), there are 345 languages and dialects reflected in the following list—and every phrase means "I love you." (Please keep in mind that the spellings of the phrases have been what might be called "Americanized" due to the profound differences in the various alphabets, and also to help you to convey the sentiments at least a little more easily than could well be the case otherwise.)

Language	Americanized Spelling
Abkhazian	Sa-u-gu-ap`x-ueit'
Ainu	Etchĕm īsmoouwoh
Alakaluf	Čix a·tjala:š tau·x(l)
Albanian	Të dashurojë
Aleut	(t'ing) txin qag'axtakuqing
Algonkin	Kisakihin
Allentiak	Cu-ca-ye-quilletc-a-nen
Alsea	Lahī-xun
Amharic	Afɨk' rɨhih^u
Anang	Âmî Mú úmâ fièn
Andaqui	Fi-ansome
Anglo-Norman	Jo t´aime
Apache	Shi ingôlth-a
Apache (Western)	N`i ɳzhóo
Arabic	'Ahebbek
Arapaho	Bixa^n-th-ethen^i
Araucanian	Inche ayueymí
Armenian	Sírĕm zk´ĕz
Atakapa	Wi in lēmo
Avar	Dí-ye mun y-ól`-ula
Avestan	Azam t(h)vām čakanām
Axvax	Dede kwi^{n}l'idi mene
Ayore	Ĩmēsĕre' ua
Azerbaijani	Sani seriram
Aztec	Nimitztlaço'tla
Balūchi	Man par tarā 'āsik-ān
Bangba	Nobato owe
Basque	Maite zaitut
Bena Kanioka	Ma nêŷe we
Bengali	Ami tomake bhalo baši
Bihoro	Ku'ani 'e'aní'e-tu'askarapanna
Bikol	Namumu'ut aku sa'ima
Biloxi	I^{n}ya^{n}hi^{n}xtí
Blackfoot	Nitsikakumimm
Bodega Miwok	Kajómu 'ópu míi
Booandik	Ngatho ngooro kroamona
Breton	Me ho kar
Buin	Nĕge lo maning-ro
Bulgarian	Obíčom tĕ
Burmese	Chítte
Cambodian	Khñom s(r)alañ 'nèak
Canienga	Konoronkwa[']
Cantonese	Ngŏh òi nĕi
Carib	Kï-sano:ma-ya
Carrizo	An-quail-an
Catalán	Jo t'amo
Catawba	De·ta namu·sá're·
Cauqui, Kauke	Na hu munkima
Cayuga	Konŏnkwa[']
Ceram	Jao suka jale
Chama	Ea mia köna
Chamoro	Hu guaiya hao
Chayma	Opunuaz
Cheremis	Məj təjəm jöratem
Cherokee	Kykéyu
Cheyenne	Ne-méhotātse
Chibcha	Hycha mue tyzisuca
Chilanga	Uno ma-shaión
Chimariko	Imī`´inan
Chimu	Temeiñ tsang
Chinese (Romanized)	Wŏ ài nǐ
Chipaya	Am pekuš
Chippewa	Gizaagi'in
Chiriguano	Xe ru-s-asú
Choctaw	Chi-ahníchali
Chuàng	Kau kyai muŋ
Chumash	K-aqciiyak-lin
Chunupi	Ha klafesh-a-e
Coahuilteco	Nākakāwa
Comanche	Tsá nəꜗswá kà
Comecrudo	Anquailam
Cochiti	Šo t^s'im
Cornish	Da garaf

Costanoan	Ka mec īúsen
Cree	Kisākihitin
Crow	Di awátsiciky
Cuna	An-pe-chabúet
Czech	Miluji vás
Dagur	Yagerieini
Dameli	Ai tō k^{y}i mehr kurunum
Danish (old)	Jeg elsker dig
Danish (new)	Eg elskar dig
Delaware	K'dahoálell
Dieri	ŋjani jidna ŋjandjai
Dioy	Kou kiay meung
Dutch	Ik houd van jou
Easter Island	He haŋaráhi áu ki a kóe
Efik	Ami mà mà fí
Egyptian	Anna bahebek
Egyptian (Ancient)	Mer-á tu
English	I love you
Eskimo	Nagligivagit
Esselen	Mislayaya kolo
Estonian	Ma armastan sind
Eweńu	Ngi nunnalubba jou
Fanti	Mí dò-wu
Farsi	Tora dust midaram
Finnish	Mínä rákistan sínua
Fipa	Nene na-ku-kunda
Fox	Ketepā´nene
French	Je t'aime
Frisian	Ik hâld fan dy
Gaelic (Irish)	Mo ghradh thú
Gaelic (Scottish)	Ta gradh agam ort-sa
Garo	Aŋa naŋ-na ka:šar-a
Georgian	Me mi-q'var-kar-šen
German	Ich liebe dich
German (Pennsylvania)	Ich liewe dich
Gisiga	'í wúd'aẁ
Golo	Me dudugu bi
Gothic (Fourth Cent.)	Ik frijō puk
Greek	Sàs aghapó
Greek (Ancient)	S'agapō
Guajiro	Áishi pia tapü 'la
Guambiano	Na munda-ke-tan
Guaraní	Se o-xaɨxú
Guarao	Ine ji obonoya
Guarauno	Ine ji obonoya
Guaymi	Mo tare tie
Gujarati	Hu^n tané prem karú ču^n
Gypsy or Romany	Mándi komóva toót
Haida	Dáng di´i kuyáadaand
Hakka	Ngǎi òi ŋg
Harsūsi	Kéwrek tūk
Hausa	Ina sanki
Hawaiian	Ke aloha nei au ia 'oe
Hebrew	Aní o-hēv otah
He-miáo	Vouay sh'ly mong
Hindi	Mayŋ toojh ko pyár karta huŋ
Hittite	Ug tug assiya-mi
Hopi	Nu' ung naawakna
Huarpe	Cu-ca-ye-quilletc-a-nen
Hungarian	Szeretlék
Hupa	Sil iūw yō
Ibanag	Kayataka
Ibo	Ahurum gi nanya
Icelandic	Eg elska pig
Igbo	Ahurum gi nanya
Ilocano	'Ai'aiatinka
Indonesian	Saja tjinta padamu
Ipurina	Nu-tarata-í
Italian	Io te amo
Japanese	Ai shite imasu
Javanese	Kulô trisno
Jivaro	Yayáxmaxmwe
Kabyle	Hamlagh kém
Kaggaba	Nas ma narhlüni

Kampa	No-ninte-m-pi	Massachusett	Koowomonsh
Kanarese	Nanu ninage prithisuthēne	Mataco	Ha humin am e
Kapampangan	Kalaguran da ka	Mayan (Yucatec)	In yamaech
Karankawa	Ná-i áwa ka	Mayan (Tojólabal)	Yah=kab'iya
Khami	Kai nang (h)la'	Mayo	Enchi nacquene
Khotanese	A thām briyaā	Mbede	Me godya we
Kickapoo	Ketapaanene	Mbum	M`i jì án jí
Kiowa	'èim-ʊ̨peidldou'	Mendé	Nyá lóngo bíé
Kire	Gu ndu vusvugi	Micmac	Kesalul
Klamath	Nû witchna mish	Moanus	Yo nyamiri oi
Köggaba	Nas ma narhlüni	Mochica	Temeiñ tsang
Komi	Me tene selemta	Mohave	Wa-kavarəm
Korean	Na nŭn tangshinŭl sarang hamnida	Mohawk	Konoronhkwa
		Mohegan	Kĕ-wi-ktam-ish
Kurdish	Ašớktem	Móng Ñjúa	Kŭ ñà kâo
Kurile	Kani ane 'eci'oma'oma	Mongolian	Chimayi khairalamui
Kutenai	Ma kutsták.te's	Montagnais	Čišáčitn
Lao	K'wăi hāk chàw	Muchik	Temeiñ tsang
Latin	Ego Tē amō	Nama	Tií-ta ke saá-ts-à ra n/àm
Latvian	Es mīlu tevi	Narragansett	Cowàmmaunsh
Lendu	Má-zhi ní	Nasioi	Karādansi oto
Lingala	Nalingi yo	Navajo	Ayói noš'ní
Lithuanian	Aš myliu tave	Nayoro	Ku'ani 'e'aní ci'eramasu'an
Logo	Ma-le ami	Noptinte Yokuts	Na mam juinthsjo
Loup	Kewamanlis	Norwegian (old)	Jeg elsker deg
Macedonian	Obíčom tĕ	Norwegian (new)	Eg elskar deg
Mahican	Nia ktachwahnen	Nubian	Ai doll-is ik-kā
Malagasy	Tiako hianao	Nùng	Cáu êp mu'hng
Malay	Saya chinta awak	Obihiro	Ku'ani 'e'aní 'eci'ekátarotke'an
Malayalam	Nyan mine snehikkunū		
Mallorcan	Jò t'àm	Ojibwa	Gizaagi'in
Maltese	Inħobbok	Okinawan	Wan ne ya suki
Manchu	Bi simbe hairambi	Omaha	Tha-é-wi-gi-re
Mandarin	Wǒ ài nǐ	Oneida	Konolonkwa[']
Manx	Ta draih aym ort	Ongtong Java	'Aŋau e aloha i 'a'oe
Marathi	Mi tulá prem krto	Onondaga	Konoenkwa[']
Mari	Məj təjəm joratem	Oriya	Mu tumaku valapai

Osage	Wa-pí-a-the	Sami (Kola Peninsula)	Munn tōn såbša
Ossetic	Aez daeu uarzən	Samoan	O te alofa ya te oe
Otomi	Dimâí	Samuku	Aimecêre qua
Oyampi	Je ne tupié	San Blas	Am-pe-abeyah
Pangasinan	Inar'arótaka	Sanskrit	Aham twān sneham karomi
Pangwe	Ma džiň oa	Santee Sioux	Waśt'e cidake
Pashto	Sto sera mina	Santo Domingo	Hin šrau tsi^m
Pawnee	Sta-sta-thix-ta	Saru	Káni 'e'aní 'eci-omáp
Pé-miáo	Kao gnia ko	Saulteaux	Kiminwe:nimin
Persian	Ašəketem	Seneca	Kūnūūkhwa'
Pilippino	I niibig kita	Serbo-Croat	Ja tebe ljubim
Piro	Poxura-kattele	Shanghainese	Ngó è nù^{ng}
Polish	Ja cię kocham	Shawnee	Nenasewelemelay
Pomo	Wi mi mará	Shilha	Hemlĕkh kemm
Ponca	Uxtawithe	Shuara	Yayáxmaxmwe
Portuguese	Eu te amo	Sinhalese	Mamáə obətə́ ádre
Portuguese (Brazil)	Eu gosto de você	Sindhi	Ma tosá piar kərianto
Potawatomi	Ksāk'ən	Sioux	Ťechi ́híla
Powhatan	Cuwumonais	Skoffie	Chacheheeten
Proto-Eastern Algonquian	Ko'wama'nethe	Slovak	Milujem ťa
Puelche	Cu-ca-ye-quilletc-a-nen	Slovenian	Rad te imam
Puget Salish	La'b čax^w d^{a}sxàtl'	Snoqualmie-Duwamish	Xa´tl'tubicidčəd
Puinave	Manté	Somali	Wankudjǎ'alahai
Punjabi	Mae^n tuanu piar krdə hə^n	Spanish	Yo te amo
Purúborá	Unubiká	Sumerian*	Ki-ma-ra-ág-en
Quechua	Kuyaikim	Suquamish	Čn ua Xi'-s-tumi
Quinnipiac	Kowômarrush	Swahili	Mimi nakupenda
Quitemoca	Imacitiakon abum	Swedish	Jag älskar dig
Quiripi	Kowômarrush	Tacana	Miza ema ebunia
Raichishka	Ku'ani 'e'ani 'eciraanuh	Tagálog	Minámahál kita
Riff	Takhsakh sham	Taiwanese	Ngùa ài dì
Rumanian	Eu te inbesc	Tamazight	Hamlay kǎi
Russian (Romanized)	Ya tebya liubliu	Tamil	Nān unei nēsikirēn
Russian (White)	Lyooblyoo ts^{y}ibyě	Tangut	Nga na ndu-vie
Saka	A thām briyaā	Tarascan	Hî-quini pampz-ca-ha-ca
Sakhalin	An-e-omap	Tasmanian	Mena coyetea nena
Sami (Kautokeino)	Mun ráhkistan du	Taulil	Ga timerek gig

Telegu	Nēnu ninnu prēmistunnānu	Yaqui	Enchi nacquene
Telei	Něge lo maning-ro	Yaunde	Ma ding oamen
Tereno	Ayaṅguatipi	Yavitero	Nutateja
Tewa	Wísígí	Yiddish	Ich libe dich
Tewa (San Juan)	Hângho wídâ	Yoruba	Muféraré
Thai	Pom rak khun	Yugoslavian	Ja te volim
Tibetan	Khyod-la čags-so	Yukaghir	Met'té tul'yo´uleǐle
Tigrinya	Yetkreki	Yuki	Li miit huc
Timucua	Chi-hobasotala	Yuncan	Temeiñ tsang
Tiv	M sọ u	Zamuco	Aimecêre gua
Tlingit	Waǐx sa xa´nisa	Zapotec (Yalalag)	Naa ranasi-a lui
Tokharian	Larem-ci	Zapotec (Istmo)	Naa Ranaxhi-a lii
Tuareg	Nek hamlakh xeum	Žu'Hòãsì (Dzu/´Oãsì)	Mí n/ām-à
Tupe	Na huma yuyq´´-ima	Zulu	Ngi ya thandela wena
Tupi	Ru-saiçú	Zuñi	Tom ho´ ichema
Turkish	Seni severim	Zyrian	Me tene selemta
Ubykh	Si-gi w-a-qə-n		
Ugaritic	iḥb-k		
Ukranian	Ya vas kokháyu		
Urdu	Mujhé tum se muhəbbət hē		
Ute	Ümi-en acendi		
Uzbek	Sizni seva-man		
Vietnamese	Anh yêu em		
Visayan	Gihǔgugmə ko 'ikaw		
Wampanóag	Koowomonnush		
Warao	Ine ji obonoya		
Wayú	Áishi pia tapü'la		
Welsh	Rwy'n dy garu di		
Wendish	Ja će lubuju		
Winnebago	Wónígeḣate		
Witoto	Odueruíteke		
Wolof	Biġina liko		
Wyandot	Yu-now-moi-e		
/Xam Bushman	N tãn a		
Yakima	A-tawish sha-mush		
Yakumo	Ku'aní 'e'aní a-'e-'omáp		
Yao	Yia nhâm mèi		

Iche liebe dich. Je t'aime. Yo te amo. Otherwise anyway you say it, "I love you."

By finding unique ways to say "I love you," you will *truly* deserve to be thought of as a "romantic!"

Charles Boyer, one of the Silver Screen's most popular leading men, had a lifetime love affair with Patricia, his wife of forty-four years. The depth of their love transcended everything that Hollywood stood for. When she died in his arms, he said, "Her love was life to me." He died just two days later, of a broken heart.

Writing Love Letters

Why write love letters? Because they make every day a special occasion by allowing you to put your passion into words, creating a whole new avenue by which to court your loved one and give an intimate gift that will always be treasured. They are declarations of love, caring, and—yes—commitment. In fact, love letters are, without a doubt, the purest gift from the heart you can give to the one you love. A gift you should give often.

Love letters allow you to take the time to choose your words carefully so as to select the right phrase or expression that lets your special someone know how special he or she is to you, and how glad you are that he or she is part of your life.

A love letter can be a short note, a long message, a poem, or anything else that, though written, includes, as it were, a part of you in it. It should be personal, giving, loving, and possibly teasing—but should always reflect the way you speak. When your loved one reads your love letter, you want him or her to "see" you, to be thinking of how much he or she cares for you, imagining that you are there in person, speaking in soft, quiet tones—wooing with tender words of love and giving emotional warmth and security.

Writing a love letter is not always easy. Especially at first. You need to give some thought to what you want to say and why you want to say it (sometimes the wrong choice of words can be damaging). You need to be in the right frame of mind to ensure that everything you are writing is relaxed and comfortable, yet fairly brimming over with your thoughts about the one you love.

The best setting in which to write a love letter is one wherein there will be no interruptions. A private place that you find comfortable, cozy, and inspiring. A place where you can have soft, relaxing background music and be surrounded by things that remind you of your loved one: her or his picture, a special gift, something with the soft scent of her perfume or his cologne—anything that focuses your attention.

Your missive can be very simple, as long as it is delivered properly. As a rule, however, your love letters should be more than just short notes. They should be personal reminders of who you are and what you are thinking, and should involve sharing. A love letter is the emissary of the secrets you share together, personal revelations of what you truly feel about each other.

If you saw a movie or a sunset or a beautiful painting that affected you emotionally, or if something happened to you that made you happy or sad, share it. Bring your sweetheart into your soul and heart and let that loved one know that when you are together your guard is always down and the door is always open.

If something (not _someone_) reminds you of your beloved, express it. Share the things about her/him that you love most—the smile, the laugh, the wonderful effect on others as well as on yourself.

Tease your loved one. Mention that you have a surprise gift, or a wonderful evening planned, or anything else special that will surely bring messages in return as he or she wonders what you are up to. But don't tell him or her any more than anyone might need to know about such things as the dress code required for an occasion, the time frame, and the like.

Always, always take the time to write _right_. Your love letters' content will lose much of its effectiveness if you try to take shortcuts (which your beloved most certainly will notice). If you must, write rough drafts, and then rewrite. Nothing is more disconcerting or destructive to the reading mood you are trying to establish than making someone decipher ramblings and corrections.

Once in a while, for a pleasant change of pace, find an appropriate musical card and write your declarations of love in it. Your lover will be serenaded as it is read. Or send a particularly meaningful card with a dab of your favorite fragrance on it as a way of helping your lover to visualize you as your words of love are read. (This may seem a cliché, but it is in fact a tried-and-true method!) Or write on a piece of parchment, wrap it around a single red rose, tie it with red ribbon, and leave it on your love's pillow, dinner plate, or car seat. Or give it to him or her at breakfast, so you'll be thought of all day long.

One especially effective and delightful approach involves a bit of pomp and circumstance: Have a gift delivered, perhaps with a specially chosen floral arrangement or a "bouquet" of helium-filled balloons, by special messenger. The gift could be a "new-found friend," such as a stuffed teddy bear. Every time your lover holds (or even looks at) the cute little animal, he or she will think warm thoughts of you.

You might find it convenient, in an office setting, to arrange for your special gift to be left on your love's desk after he or she leaves work for the day, so that your accompanying message, read first thing in the morning, generates wonderful thoughts and feelings that remain all day long—reminders of how wonderful you are. What a way to set the stage for a special evening!

Creativity is the key.

Besides the enchantment of the love letter, your special someone will have the memory of how it arrived. And, as an added bonus, the mind, which is a marvelously creative force, will continually enhance the recollection of what you sent to the point that it becomes even more meaningful over time.

The written word, perhaps more than any other means of expression, adds a special touch to love, romance, and the quest for happiness. Accompanied by a timely and thoughtful gift or shared event, it can create an impression that will linger long in shared memories.

Sending Love Poetry

 poem, especially when part of a love letter, is a wonderful way to tell someone "I love you." In fact, poetry itself is the ultimate love letter, at the same time enchanting and effective.

Just as with a love letter, the content of every poem you send is important. You must write or select poetry that expresses what you are feeling; your loved one must feel it came from you.

Since verse written in Old English loses its promise and effectiveness for contemporary couples, you might try to write one of your own poems in Modern English—or whichever other tongue you can use well. In addition to knowing it came from you, your loved one will have the additional pleasure of reading words from your heart rather than from someone else's.

Poetry from your heart can express the joy and love that your special someone has brought into your life—as I have done in these excerpts from some of my personal poetry:

> *Beautiful dreams*
> *coming through;*
> *loving realities,*
> *enchantment true.*

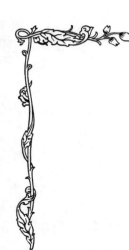

Sanguine paradise,
Utopia new;
breathless impatience,
dreaming of you.

Bringing lives together,
defining lifetime roles;
sowing loving feelings,
mending troubled souls.

Touching without holding,
giving love its sheen;
thanking God I met you,
beauty truly seen!

Or, it can simply state what you feel, as this excerpt does:

I love
your gentle touch
caressing my hand,
guiding my heart
persuasively.

I love
your breath against my neck
as we dance,
moving to our feelings
rhythmically.

I love
the scent of your perfume
as it lingers,
floating in the air
intoxicatingly.

Finally, your poems don't have to be long. All they need be are reminders of you. There is even poetry in a prose sentence like "I am truly grateful for the love, caring, and strength your love has brought into my life!"

If you're not comfortable about writing a poem of your own, you can always choose one of the all-time great love poems, such as the following.

How Do I Love Thee?

(From _Sonnets from the Portuguese_, No. 43)
by Elizabeth Barrett Browning

How do I love thee? Let me count the ways.
I love thee to the depth and breadth and height
My soul can reach, when feeling out of sight
For the ends of Being and ideal Grace.
I love thee to the level of every day's
Most quiet need, by sun and candlelight.
I love thee freely, as men strive for Right;
I love thee purely, as they turn from Praise.
I love thee with the passion put to use
    In my old griefs, and with my childhood's faith.
I love thee with a love I seemed to lose
    With my lost saints—I love thee with the breath,
Smiles, tears, of all my life!— and, if God choose,
    I shall but love thee better after death.

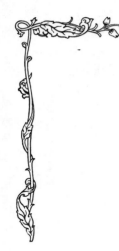

Shall I Compare Thee to a Summer's Day?
(Sonnet XVIII)
by William Shakespeare

Shall I compare thee to a summer's day?
Thou art more lovely and more temperate.
Rough winds do shake the darling buds of May,
And summer's lease hath all too short a date.
Sometime too hot the eye of heaven shines,
And often is his gold complexion dimm'd;
And every fair from fair sometime declines,
By chance or nature's changing course, untrimm'd;
But thy eternal summer shall not fade
Nor lose possession of that fair thou ow'st,
Nor shall Death drag thou wand'rest in his shade
When in eternal lines to time thou grow'st.
    So long as men can breathe or eyes can see,
    So long lives this, and this gives life to thee.

To Delia
(Sonnet No. 1)
by Samuel Daniel

Unto the boundless ocean of thy beauty
Runs this poor river, charg'd with streams of zeal:
Returning thee the tribute of my duty,
Which here my love, my youth, my plaints reveal.
Here I unclasp the book of my chrg'd soul,
Where I have cast th'accounts of all my care:
Here have I summ'd my sighs, here I enroll
How they were spent for thee; look what they are.

Look on the dear expenses of my youth,
And see how just I reckon with thine eyes:
Examine well thy beauty with my truth,
And cross my cares ere greater sums arise.
        Read it, sweet maid, though it be done but slightly;
        Who can show all his love, doth love but lightly.

Summer Night

by Alfred, Lord Tennyson

Nor sleeps the crimson petal, now the white;
Nor waves the cypress in the palace walk;
Nor winks the gold fin in the porphyry font:
The firefly wakens: waken thou with me.

Now droops the milk-white peacock like a ghost,
And like a ghost she glimmers on to me.

Now lies the Earth all Danaë to the stars,
And all thy heart lies open unto me.

Now slides the silent meteor on, and leaves
A shining furrow, as thy thoughts in me.

Now folds the lily all her sweetness up,
And slips into the bosom of the lake:
So fold thyself, my dearest, thou, and slip
Into my bosom and be lost in me.

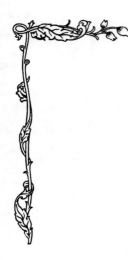

The Passionate Shepherd to His Love
by Christopher Marlowe

Come live with me and be my Love,
And we will all the pleasures prove
That valleys, groves, hills and fields,
Woods, or steepy mountain yields.

And we will sit upon the rocks,
Seeing the shepherds feed their flocks
By shallow rivers, to whose falls
Melodious birds sing madrigals.

And I will make thee beds of roses,
And a thousand fragrant posies;
A cap of flowers, and a kirtle,
Embroider'd all with leaves of myrtle.

A gown made of the finest wool
Which from our pretty lambs we pull,
Fair-lined slippers for the cold,
With buckles of the purest gold.

A belt of straw and ivy-buds,
With coral clasps and amber studs,
And if these pleasures may thee move,
Come live with me, and be my Love.

The shepherd swains shall dance and sing
For thy delight each May-morning.
If these delights thy mind may move,
Then live with me, and be my Love.

Love Bade Me Welcome
by George Herbert

Love bade me welcome; yet my soul drew back,
    Guilty of dust and sin.
But quick-eyed Love, observing me grow slack
    From my first entrance in,
Drew nearer to me, sweetly questioning
    If I lacked any thing.

"A guest," I answered, "worthy to be here."
    Love said, "You shall be he."
"I the unkind, ungrateful? Ah my dear,
    I cannot look on thee."
Love took my hand, and smiling did reply,
    "Who made the eyes but I?"

"Truth Lord, but I have marred them; let my shame
    Go where it doth deserve."
"And know you not," says Love, "who bore the blame?
    My dear, then I will serve.
You must sit down," says Love, "and taste my meat."
    So I did sit and eat.

    One final word of advice: whether you send love notes, love letters, or love poems, send something of yourself as part of each. Those loving, tender treasures will be instrumental in building a future for both of you to enjoy and savor—so let your true feelings flow, be honest about who you are, and share your dreams and aspirations freely.

The Language of Flowers

Flowers are nature's way of letting us know that all's well with the world and that love's season is always in full bloom.

The wonderful and inspiring practice of giving flowers to express love and caring originated in the Orient. By the 1600s, flowers had gained a special symbolism as a way for lovers even in faraway Constantinople to communicate with each other without ever having to say a word, thus adding a whole new dimension to the art of romance and love.

The true beauty of flowers is that they have a "language" all their own! In fact, that language was introduced to the Western world in the early 1700s, compliments of Lady Mary Wortley Montagu, a socially celebrated British letter-writer and poet. She happened upon it while married to the British ambassador to the Turkish Court (in Constantinople), and wrote about it to her friends—thereby causing an instant stir. The French, with their reputation for romance, quickly took up this wonderful custom as well, and at that point it was only a matter of time before members of polite society all over Europe were speaking of love via flowers. So it is clear that flowers, as an expression of love and affection, have been a part of many a culture for a very long time.

Today, thanks to this enchanting custom, there are over eight hundred flowers (including in that category plants, herbs, and fruits) whose special meaning—or meanings—can add great pleasure to both romance and love.

In addition to surprising your lover with flowers, you can incorporate their meanings into a love letter. Your message might say, "I offer true friendship (oak-leaved geranium), affection (gillyflower, better known as carnation), and devotion (heliotrope)." By sending an arrangement of eleven red roses ("passionate love") and one—signifying "one of a kind"—lavender rose ("pure love"), you could tell your loved one, "You are one of a kind, and my love for you is true." Similarly, a bouquet of lily-of-the-valleys ("Let's forgive and be happy again") can be used as a peace offering after a lover's quarrel. Besides being beautiful and delicate, they are wonderfully fragrant.

Since the possibilities of communicating through flowers are endless, you can easily find other unique ways to woo with them, such as:

♥ Leave a single red rose on your lover's pillow, attached to a hand-written love note.

♥ Bring your loved one a flower a day (not the same kind very often) for thirty days before his or her birthday (or some other special-to-your-mate occasion). He or she will soon have an ever-changing arrangement that will be both a constant delight and a continual reminder of how special you are.

♥ Send an arrangement of fragrant flowers that will surround your companion with wonderful scents and thoughts of you—but first make sure that he or she is not allergic to them, or else the thoughts evoked may not be the ones you wanted to stimulate. Possibilities here include gardenias, lilacs, lillies, roses—especially Prelude (mauve/lilac) and Preview (white)—and tuberoses. Your florist may have other suggestions as well.

♥ Give an arrangement of edible flowers, such as marigolds, pineapple sage, rose-scented geraniums, tiger lilies, zucchini flowers, or some herbs you've grown or picked yourself, in a basket. You might even include some creative recipes.

♥ Send him or her an exotic plant. It can grow right along with your relationship!

By using your imagination in creative ways to court your loved one with flowers, you will be appreciated all the more for having taken the time to shower her/him with your affections.

Which flower-borne words of love would you use to tell your sweetheart how special he or she is to you?

Flower	Thought Expressed
Acacia	Chaste love
Acacia (Pink)	Elegance
Acacia (Rose)	Friendship, platonic love
Acacia (Yellow)	Secret love
Acanthus	Artifice, the fine arts
Aloe	Religious superstition
Allspice	Compassion
Almond (Flowering)	Hope
Almond Tree	Indiscretion
Alyssum (Sweet)	Worth beyond beauty
Amaranth	Immortality
Amaranth (Globe)	Unfading love
Amaryllis	Pride, splendid beauty, timidity
Ambrosia	Love returned
Amethyst	Admiration
Anemone	Expectation, sickness
Anemone (Garden)	Forsaken
Angelica	Inspiration
Apple	Temptation
Apple Blossom	Preference
Ash Tree	Grandeur
Ash (Mountain)	Prudence
Aspen Tree	Lamentation
Aster	Variety
Aster (China)	Variety
Auricula	Importune me not
Auricula (Scarlet)	Avarice
Azalea	Temperance; love; romance
Baby's Breath Posies	Gentleness, everlasting love
Bachelor's Buttons	Single blessedness
Balm	Sympathy
Balm of Gilead	Cure
Balsam	Ardent love
Balsam (Red)	Impatient yet resolved to win your love
Balsam (Yellow)	Impatience
Barberry	Sharpness
Basil (Common)	Hatred
Basil (Sweet)	Good wishes
Bay Leaf	Consistency, I change but in death
Bay Tree	Glory
Bay Wreath	Reward of merit
Beech Tree	Prosperity
Begonia	Dark thoughts
Bell Flower	Gratitude
Belladonna	Silence
Bindweed (Great)	Insinuation
Bindweed (Small)	Humility
Birch Tree	Gracefulness, meekness
Bittersweet	Truth
Bluebell	Constancy
Borage	Bluntness
Box Tree	Stoicism

Lady Mary Wortley Montagu, *the previously cited socially cele-brated British letter-writer and poet, once found, during her stay in Istanbul, a Turkish love letter that interpreted the meanings of various flowers, herbs, and plants. She was so fas-cinated by it that she sent copies to friends in European society, suggesting that it would allow lovers to secretly communicate without "inking the fingers."*

Bramble	Envy, lowliness, remorse	Celandine	Joys to come
Broom	Humility, neatness	Cherry (White)	Deception
Buttercup	Childishness, ingratitude	Cherry Blossom	Spiritual beauty
Cabbage	Gain	Cherry Tree	Education
Camellia	Steadfast love	Chervil (Garden)	Sincerity
Camellia Japonica	Unpretending excellence	Chestnut Tree (Sweet)	Do me justice
Camellia Japonica (White)	Perfected loveliness	Chickweed	Rendezvous
Camomile	Energy in adversity	Chives	Usefulness
Campanula	Gratitude	Chrysanthemum (Red)	I love
Canary Grass	Perseverence	Chrysanthemum (White)	Truth
Candytuft	Indifference	Chrysanthemum (Yellow)	Slighted love
Canterbury Bell	Acknowledgment	Cinquefoil	Maternal affection
Caraway	Betrayal	Clematis	Mental beauty
Cardinal Flower	Distinction	Clematis (Evergreen)	Poverty
Carnation	Fascination, burning love, woman's love	Clover (Four-Leafed)	Be mine
Carnation (Red)	Alas, my poor heart	Clover (White)	Think of me
Carnation (Striped)	Refusal	Cloves	Dignity
Carnation (Yellow)	Disdain	Cockscomb	Singularity
Cedar	Strength	Coltsfoot	Justice shall be done to you
Cedar Leaf	I live for thee	Columbine	Folly
Cedar of Lebanon	Incorruptible	Columbine (Purple)	Resolution

Columbine (Red)	Anxious; trembling
Convolvulus	Uncertainty; bonds
Convolvulus (Major)	Extinguished hopes
Convolvulus (Minor)	Night
Coriander	Concealed merit
Coreopsis	Always cheerful
Corn	Riches
Cornflower	Delicacy
Cowslip	Pensiveness, winning grace
Cowslip (American)	Divine beauty
Cranberry	Cure for heartache
Crane's Bill	Envy
Cress	Power
Crocus (Spring)	Youthful gladness
Currant	Thy frown will kill me
Currants (Branch of)	You please all
Cyclamen	Diffidence
Cypress	Death, despair, melancholy, mourning
Daffodil	Regard
Daffodil (Gret Yellow)	Chivalry
Dahlia	Good taste, instability
Daisy	Innocence
Daisy (Michaelmas)	Afterthought
Daisy (Ox-eye)	A token
Daisy (Parti-Colored)	Beauty
Daisy (Red)	Unconscious
Daisy (White)	Innocence
Dandelion	Love's oracle, rustic oracle
Dill	Good spirits
Dittany (White)	Passion
Dock	Patience

Dogsbane	Deceit
Dogwood	Durability
Eglantine	Poetry
Elder	Zealousness
Eupatorium	Delay
Everlasting Pea	Appointed meeting
Fennel	Strength
Fern	Sincerity
Fern (Flowering)	Reverie
Fig	Argument, longevity
Filbert	Reconciliation
Fir (Scotch)	Elevation
Flax	Fate, I feel your kindness
Fleur-de-Lis	Flame
Fleur-de-Luce	Fire
Flytrap	Deceit
Forget-Me-Not	True love; fond remember ance; forget-me-not
Foxglove	Insincerity, a wish
French Honeysuckle	Rustic beauty
Fuchsia (Scarlet)	Taste
Gardenia	A secret love
Gentian	You are unjust
Geranium	Expected meeting
Geranium (Dark)	Melancholy
Geranium (Ivy)	I engage you for the next dance
Geranium (Lemon)	Unexpected meeting
Geranium (Oak-Leaved)	True friendship
Geranium (Pencil-Leaved)	Ingenuity
Geranium (Rose-Scented)	Preference
Geranium (Scarlet)	Comforting

Geranium (Silver-Leaved)	Recall
Geranium (Wild)	Steadfast piety
Gillyflower	Lasting and/or unfading beauty; bonds of affection
Gladiola	Strong character
Gloxinia	A proud spirit
Golden Rod	Precaution
Gooseberry	Anticipation
Gorse	Enduring affection
Gourd	Extent
Harebell	Grief
Hawthorn	Hope
Hazel	Reconciliation
Helenium	Tears
Heliotrope	Devotion; faithfulness
Hemlock	You will be my death
Hemp	Fate
Hibiscus	Delicate beauty
Holly	Am I forgotten?; foresight
Holly Herb	Enchantment
Hollyhock	Ambition; fecundity
Hollyhock (White)	Female ambition
Honesty	Fascination; honesty
Honey Flower	Sweet and secret love
Honeysuckle	Devoted affection
Honeysuckle (Coral)	Color of my life and/or fate
Honeysuckle (French)	Rustic beauty
Honeysuckle (Monthly)	I will not answer hastily
Honeysuckle (Wild)	Inconstancy in love
Hop	Injustice
Hornbeam Tree	Ornament
Hyacinth	Game, play

Hydrangea	Heartlessness; boastfulness
Hyssop	Cleanliness
Iceland Moss	Health
Ice Plant	Your looks will freeze me
Imperial (Crown)	Majesty
Iris	Message for you; flame; my compliments
Iris (Yellow)	Passion
Ivy	Fidelity; assiduous to please; marriage
Jacob's Ladder	Come down
Jasmine (Cape)	I am too happy; transport of joy
Jasmine (Carolina)	Separation
Jasmine (Indian)	Attachment
Jasmine (Spanish)	Sensuality
Jasmine (White)	Amiability
Jasmine (Yellow)	Grace; elegance
Jonquil	Desiring a return of affection
Judas Tree	Unbelief
Laburnum	Pensive beauty; forsaken
Lady's Mantle	Fashion
Lady's Slipper	Capricious beauty; Win me and wear me
Lantana	Rigor
Larkspur	Lightness; levity
Larkspur (Pink)	Fickleness
Larkspur (Purple)	Haughtiness
Laurel	Glory
Laurel (Mountain)	Ambition
Laurestina	A token; I die if neglected
Lavender	Distrust
Lavender (Sea)	Dauntlessness

Lemon	Zest
Lemon Blossom	Discretion; fidelity in love
Lichen	Dejection
Lilac (Field)	Humility
Lilac (Purple)	Love's first emotions
Lilac (White)	Youthful innocence; modesty; purity
Lilac Polyanthus	Confidence
Lily (Arum)	Ardor
Lily (Imperial)	Majesty
Lily (White)	Sweetness; modesty; purity
Lily (Yellow)	Falsehood; gaiety
Lily Of The Valley	Return of happiness; Let's forgive and be happy again
Lime	Conjugal love
Liquorice	I declare against you
Lobelia	Malevolence
Lotus Flower	Estranged love
Love-in-a-Mist	Perplexity
Love-Lies-Bleeding	Hopeless but not heartless
Lucerne	Life
Lupine	Voraciousness, imagination
Maidenhair	Discretion

Magnolia	Love of nature
Magnolia (Laurel-Leaved)	Dignity
Magnolia (Swamp)	Perseverance
Maple	Reserve
Marigold	Grief; despair; melancholy
Marigold (African)	Vulgar-minded
Marigold (French)	Jealousy
Marigold (Prophetic)	Prediction
Marjoram	Blushing
Meadowsweet	Uselessness
Mercury	Goodness
Mignonette	Your qualities surpass your charms
Mimosa	Sensitiveness
Mint	Virtue; wisdom
Mistletoe	I surmount difficulties
Mock Orange	Counterfeit
Morning Glory	Affectation
Moss	Maternal love
Mossy Saxifrage	Affection
Motherwort	Concealed love
Mugwort	Happiness
Mulberry (Black)	I will not survive you

The hand with which flowers are given and received further defines the meaning of the gift. The right hand indicates a positive wish, the left hand a negative one.

Mulberry (White)	Wisdom	Pea (Everlasting)	Lasting pleasure; an appointed meeting
Mushroom	Suspicion	Pea (Sweet)	Lasting pleasure; departure
Mustard Seed	Indifference	Peach	Your qualities, like your charms, are unequaled
Myrrh	Gladness		
Myrtle	Love	Peach Blossom	I am your captive
Narcissus	Egotism	Pear and Pear Blossom	Affection
Narcissus (Poet's)	Self-esteem	Pear (Prickly)	Satire
Nasturtium	Patriotism	Pennyroyal	Flee away
Nettle (Stinging)	Slander	Peony	Bashfulness; shame
Nightshade	Witchcraft	Peppermint	Warmth of feeling; cordiality
Nightshade (Woody)	Truth	Periwinkle (Blue)	Early friendship
Nosegay	Gallantry	Periwinkle (White)	Pleasant recollections
Nutmeg	Expected meeting	Persicaria	Restoration
Oak Leaves	Bravery	Petunia	Don't despair
Oak Tree	Hospitality	Phlox	Unanimity
Oak Tree (White)	Independence	Pimpernel	Assignation; change
Oats	Music	Pine	Pity
Oleander	Beware	Pine (Spruce)	Hope in adversity
Olive Branch	Peace	Pineapple	Welcome
Orange and Orange Tree	Generosity	Pink	Boldness
Orange Blossoms	Your purity equals your loveliness	Pink (Carnation)	Woman's love
		Pink (Double Red)	Pure and ardent love
Orchid	A beauty	Pink (Indian Double)	Always lovely
Orchid (Butterfly)	Gaiety	Pink (Indian Single)	Aversion
Ox Eye	Patience	Pink (Single Red)	Pure love
Palm	Victory	Pink (Variegated)	Refusal
Pansy	Thinking good thoughts of you	Pink (White)	Talent
		Plane Tree	Genius
Parsley	Festivity; feasting; useful knowledge	Plum Tree	Keep your promises
		Plum Tree (Wild)	Independence
Parsley (Fool's)	Silliness	Polyanthus	Pride of riches
Passionflower	Belief; religious superstition; susceptibility		

Polyanthus (Crimson)	The heart's mystery
Pomegranate	Foolishness
Pomegranate Flower	Mature elegance
Poplar (White)	Time
Poppy	Evanescent pleasure
Poppy (Red)	Consolation
Poppy (Scarlet)	Fantastic extravagance
Poppy (White)	Sleep
Primrose	Early youth
Primrose (Evening)	Inconstancy
Primula	Diffidence
Quince	Temptation
Ranunculus	You are radiant with charms
Ranunculus (Wild)	Ingratitude
Raspberry	Remorse
Reeds	Music
Rhododendron	Danger
Rhubarb	Advice
Robin (Ragged)	Wit
Rocket	Rivalry
Rose	Love
Rose (Austrian)	Thou art all that is lovely
Rose (Bridal)	Happy love
Rose (Burgundy)	Unconscious beauty
Rose (Cabbage)	Ambassador of love
Rose (Campion)	Only deserve my love
Rose (Carolina)	Love is dangerous
Rose (China)	Beauty always new
Rose (Christmas)	Please relieve my anxiety
Rose (Coral)	Admiration for your accomplishments and talents
Rose (Daily)	I aspire to your smile

Rose (Damask)	Brilliant complexion; freshness
Rose (Deep Red)	Bashful shame
Rose (Dog)	Pleasure and pain
Rose (Guelder)	Age; winter
Rose (Lavender)	Pure love
Rose (May)	Precocity
Rose (Multiflora)	Grace
Rose (Mundi)	Variety
Rose (Musk)	Capricious beauty
Rose (Pink)	Friendship; graceful beauty
Rose (Pompom)	Prettiness
Rose (Provence)	My heart is in flames
Rose (Red)	Passion; beauty
Rose (Red-Leaved)	Beauty and prosperity
Rose (Red and White Together)	Unity
Rose (Thornless)	Early attachment
Rose (Unique)	Call me not beautiful
Rose (White)	Purity; the giver is worthy of your love
Rose (Withered White)	Transient impressions
Rose (Yellow)	Jealousy; decrease in love
Rose (York)	War
Rosebud (Moss)	Confession of love
Rosebud (Red)	Pure and lovely; You are young and beautiful
Rosebud (White)	A heart ignorant of love; girlhood
Rosemary	Rememberance; Your presence revives me
Roses (Garland of)	Reward of virtue
Rue	Disdain
Sage	Domestic virtue

Sage (Garden)	Esteem
Saffron	Beware of excess; Do not abuse our relationship
Saffron (Meadow)	My best days are past
Salvia (Blue)	I think of you
Salvia (Red)	Forever thine
Savory	Boldness
Scabious	Unfortunate love
Scabious (Sweet)	Widowhood
Scilla (Blue)	Forgive and forget
Snapdragon	No; presumption
Snowdrop	Hope
Sorrel	Affection; parental affection
Sorrel (Wood)	Joy; maternal tenderness
Southernwood	Bantering; jest
Spearmint	Warmth of sentiment
Speedwell	Female fidelity
Spiked Willow Herb	Pretension
Spiderwort	Esteem (without love)
Starwort (American)	Cheerfulness in old age
Stephanotis	You can boast too much
Stock	Lasting beauty
Stock (Ten-Week)	Promptness
Stonecrop	Tranquility
Straw	Agreement
Straw (Broken)	Rupture of a contract
Strawberry	Perfect elegance
Strawberry Tree	Esteem (with love)
Sunflower (Dwarf)	Adoration
Sunflower (Tall)	Haughtiness
Swallow-Wort	Cure for heartache
Sweet Basil	Good wishes
Sweetbrier (American)	Simplicity
Sweetbrier (Yellow)	Decrease of love
Sweet Flag	Fitness
Sweet William	Gallantry; a smile; finesse
Sycamore	Curiosity
Syringa	Memory
Syringa (Carolina)	Disappointment
Tamarisk	Crime
Taragon	Unselfishness
Tendrils of Climbing Plants	Ties
Thistle (Scotch)	Retaliation
Thorn Apple	Deceitful charms
Thorns (Branch of)	Severity
Thrift	Sympathy
Thyme	Activity; thriftiness
Toothwort	Secret love
Traveler's Joy	Safety
Tree of Life	Old age
Trefoil (Birdsfoot)	Revenge
Trillium Pictum	Modest beauty
Truffle	Surprise
Trumpet Flower	Fame
Tuberose	Dangerous pleasures
Tulip	Fame
Tulip (Red)	Declaration of love
Tulip (Variegated)	Beautiful eyes
Tulip (Yellow)	Hopeless love
Turnip	Charity
Verbena (White)	Pure; guileless
Veronica	Fidelity
Vetch	Shyness
Violet (Blue)	Faithfulness; love

Violet (Dame)	Watchfulness	Willow (Weeping)	Mourning
Violet (Purple)	You occupy my thoughts	Wisteria	Welcome
Violet (White)	Innocence; modesty	Woodbine	Fraternal love
Violet (Wild)	Love in idleness	Wormwood	Absence
Violet (Yellow)	Rural happiness	Yew	Sadness
Virgin's Bower	Filial love	Zephyr Flower	Sickness
Wallflower	Fidelity in adversity	Zinnia	Thoughts of an absent friend
Wheat	Prosperity		
Willow (Creeping)	Forsaken love		
Willow (Water)	Freedom	Flowers keep romance alive!	

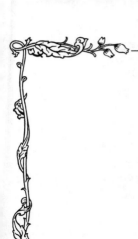

The Gift of Music

One of the most sentimental and romantic gifts that you can give your loved one is the gift of music, which offers an enormous range of possibilities. It can be a tune from the year or decade in which your lover was born, a ballad that has a particular message you want to send, music that sets a particular mood, or "your song." It can be a song about love and romance or one named after your sweetheart—perhaps as in the following list.

Song	Performer
"You Can Call Me Al"	Paul Simon
"Alfie"	Cher
"Alice"	Stevie Nicks
"Alisha"	Chet Atkins
"Alison"	Elvis Costello
"Amanda"	Boston
"Amie"	Pure Prairie League
"Amy"	Percy Faith
"Anastasia"	Pat Boone
"Andy"	Mothers of Invention
"Angelia"	Richard Marx

"Angie"	The Rolling Stones	"Eddie My Love"	Teen Queens
"Anna"	The Beatles	"Elaine"	Smithereens
"Annie's Song"	John Denver	"Eleanor"	Turtles
"Annie"	From the musical *Annie*	"Eli's Coming"	Three Dog Night
"Arthur's Theme"	Christopher Cross	"Elvira"	Oak Ridge Boys
"Aubrey"	Bread	"Evangeline"	The Band
"Barbara Ann"	Beach Boys	"Eve"	Carpenters
"Ben"	Michael Jackson	"Felicia"	Herb Alpert
"Beth"	Kiss	"Fernando"	ABBA
"Beth"	Maurice Jarre	"Francene"	ZZ Top
"Bill"	The Fifth Dimension	"Frankie"	Connie Francis
"Billie Jean"	Michael Jackson	"Gina"	Johnny Mathis
"Bobbie Sue"	Oak Ridge Boys	"Gloria"	The Doors
"Bobby Jean"	Bruce Springsteen	"Harry"	Janis Joplin
"Bruce"	Rick Springfield	"Hey Paula"	Paul and Paula
"Carl of the Jungle"	Rick Nelson	"Hurrah for Christopher"	Lesley Adams
"Oh Carol"	Neil Sedaka	"Jane"	Starship
"Cecilia"	Simon and Garfunkel	"Jean"	Oliver
"Cherie"	Steve Perry	"Jennifer Juniper"	Donovan
"Chloe"	Elton John	"Jesse"	Roberta Flack
"Cindy, Oh, Cindy"	Eddie Fisher	"Jill"	Harry Conick, Jr.
"Claudette"	The Everly Brothers	"Joanna"	Kool and the Gang
"Cracklin' Rosie"	Neil Diamond	"Joey"	Natalie Cole
"Daniel"	Elton John	"Johnny B. Goode"	Chuck Berry
"David"	John McLaughlin	"Johnny Angel"	The Carpenters
"Dear Prudence"	The Beatles	"Johnny Loves Me"	Shelley Fabares
"Denise"	Randy and the Rainbows	"Jolene"	Dolly Parton
"Desiree"	Neil Diamond	"Josie"	Steely Dan
"Diana"	Paul Anka	"Judy"	The Dorsey Brothers
"Donna"	Richie Valens	"Julia"	The Beatles
"Dream Boat Annie"	Heart	"Julie, Do Ya Love Me?"	Bobby Sherman
"Duncan"	Paul Simon	"Kevin's Song"	Goo Goo Dolls

"Think of Laura"	Christopher Cross
"Layla"	Eric Clapton
"Leah"	Roy Orbison
"Linda"	Jan and Dean
"Lucille"	Little Richard
"Lucy in the Sky With Diamonds"	The Beatles
"Mandy"	Barry Manilow
"Mary Lou"	Robbie Nevil
"Mary, Mary"	Hi-Five
"Mary Ruth"	Harry Conick, Jr.
"Mary's Prayer"	Danny Wilson
"Martha"	Jefferson Airplane
"Martha My Dear"	The Beatles
"Message to Michael"	Dionne Warwick
"Michael"	Joan Baez
"Michelle"	The Beatles
"My Marie"	B. W. Stevenson
"Nadine"	The Dells
"Nadine (Is It You?)"	Chuck Berry
"Natalia"	Van Morrison
"Peg"	Steely Dan
"Peggy-O"	Simon and Garfunkel
"Peggy Sue"	Buddy Holly
"Rachel and Book" (Love Theme from *Witness*)	Maurice Jarre
"Help Me Rhonda"	Beach Boys
"Lovely Rita"	The Beatles
"Roni"	Bobby Brown
"Rosalinda's Eyes"	Billy Joel
"Rosalita"	Bruce Springsteen

"Roseanna"	Toto
"Roxanne"	Police
"Sam"	Olivia Newton-John
"Sara"	Starship
"Sara Smile"	Hall and Oates
"Sarah"	Fleetwood Mac
"Sexy Sadie"	The Beatles
"Oh Sheila"	Ready for the World
"Sheila"	Tommy Roe
"Sherry"	Four Seasons
"Sheri"	Journey
"Susan"	Buckinghams
"Susie"	Elton John
"Suzanne"	Leonard Cohen
"Sweet Caroline"	Neil Diamond
"Sweet Mary"	Wadsworth Mansion
"Teddy"	Connie Francis
"Tommy Can You Hear Me?"	Peter Townshend
"Tracy"	Cuff Links
"Valarie"	The Monkees
"Valerie"	Steve Winwood
"Vera"	Pink Floyd
"Veronica"	Elvis Costello
"Victor"	Blondie
"Victoria"	Kinks
"Wendy"	Beach Boys
"Willie"	Joni Mitchell
"Yoko"	John Lennon

Or it can be one of the top twenty-five love songs of all time:

Song	Performer
"All I Ask of You"	From *Phantom of the Opera*
"All My Loving"	The Beatles
"Bolero"	Maurice Ravel
"Chances Are"	Johnny Mathis
"Endless Love"	Diana Ross and Lionel Richie
"Have I Told You Lately That I Love You?"	Van Morrison
"Kisses Sweeter Than Wine"	Pat Boone
"Lara's Theme"	From *Dr. Zhivago*
"Little Fall of Rain"	From *Les Miserables*
"Looks Like We Made It"	Barry Manilow
"Love Is a Wonderful Thing"	Michael Bolton
"Love Me Tender"	Elvis Presley
"Love of My Life"	Abba
"Moon River"	Andy Williams
"Moonlight Sonata"	Ludwig van Beethoven
"No One Else on Earth"	Wynonna
"Power of Love"	Huey Lewis
"Strangers in the Night"	Frank Sinatra
"Time Love and Tenderness"	Michael Bolton
"Unchained Melody"	The Righteous Brothers
"Until the Twelfth of Never"	Johnny Mathis
"You Are the Sunshine of My Life"	Stevie Wonder
"You Don't Send Me Flowers Anymore"	Neil Diamond and Barbra Streisand
"You Lost That Loving Feeling"	The Righteous Brothers
"The Wedding Song"	Paul Stookey

You will already *know* what your loved one likes, so stop by your local music center, say what you're looking for, and let the music lead the way. (Don't forget the note saying that you are thinking about him or her!)

George Burns and Gracie Allen's theme
song was "Love Nest."

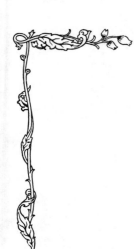

How to Send Messages With Gems

emstones not only are beautiful to behold, they also have very particular meanings when given as gifts to signify certain situations—birthdays, other special days, and the sending of unusual messages.

Precious gemstones have been used as birthstones throughout the history of humankind. The Arabians, the Babylonians, the Hebrews, the Hindus, the Italians, the Polish, the Romans, the Russians, and the Spaniards all utilized precious gems to celebrate birthdays, believing that the recipient would be brought good fortune if he or she always kept the right birthstone in or on something worn. The choice of stone was based on the assignment of the gem to the recipient's Zodiac sign.

Although the list of assigned gemstones became more or less standardized in the eighteenth and nineteenth centuries, it wasn't until the 1912 Jewelers Convention that a "modern" list was finally formalized. It was as follows:

Month	Gemstone(s)
January	Garnet
February	Amethyst
March	Aquamarine or Bloodstone
April	Diamond
May	Emerald
June	Moonstone or Pearl
July	Carnelian or Ruby
August	Peridot or Sardonyx
September	Sapphire
October	Opal or Tourmaline
November	Topaz
December	Lapis Lazuli or Turquoise

Nevertheless, many other beliefs about gemstones remained, including that a certain one worn on a particular day of the week would bring the wearer even more good fortune:

Day of the Week	Gemstone
Sunday	Ruby
Monday	Moonstone
Tuesday	Coral
Wednesday	Emerald
Thursday	Cat's Eye
Friday	Diamond
Saturday	Sapphire

Each gemstone has special meanings of its own:

Gemstone	Anniversary	Symbolization/Endowment
Agate		Endows the wearer with calmness, courage, eloquence, health, longevity, virtue, and wealth
Amethyst	February	Symbolizes deep love, happiness, humility, sincerity, and wealth
Aquamarine	March	Believed to ensure continual happiness and constancy in love; symbolizes health, hope, and youth
Beryl		Symbolizes everlasting youth, happiness, and hope
Bloodstone	March	Believed to endow courage, wisdom, and vitality; symbolizes audaciousness,brilliance, courage, generosity, and health
Carbunkle		Symbolizes constancy, energy, self- confidence, and strength
Carnelian	July	Symbolizes courage, joy, friendship, and peace; believed to disperse evil thoughts and sorrow
Cat's Eye	Thursday	Symbolizes long life and platonic love; believed to warn its owner of approaching danger
Chrysoberyl		Symbolizes patience in sorrow
Chrysolite		Symbolizes disappointed love, and wisdom
Coral	Tuesday	Symbolizes attachment; believed to be an amulet against natural disasters, disease, bad luck, and jealous friends
Crystal	15th	Symbolizes purity and simplicity
Diamond	Friday, April, 60th and 75th	Sybolizes brilliance, constancy, excellence, innocence, invulnerable faith, joy, life, love, and purity
Emerald	Wednesday, May, 55th	Symbolizes spring, rebirth, hope, peace, and tranquility; believed to endow its wearer with an accommodating and pleasing disposition

Garnet	January	Symbolizes constancy, faith, loyalty, and strength; believed to endow its wearer with cheerfulness and sincerity
Hyacinth (Jacinth)		Symbolizes modesty, constancy, hope, faithfulness, and perfection; believed to endow its wearer with "second sight"
Jade		Symbolizes harmonious living, intelligence, longevity, strength, and purity; believed to endow its wearer with good luck and good health; embodies charity, wisdom, courage, justice, and modesty
Jasper		Symbolizes courage, joy, and wisdom; believed to endow its wearer with constancy
Lapis Lazuli	December	Symbolizes ability, cheerfulness, nobility, and truth; believed to bring its wearer happiness, love, and prosperity
Moonstone	Monday June	Symbolizes pensiveness and intelligence; believed to bring its wearer good luck
Onyx		Symbolizes clearness and dignity; believed to bring its wearer marital bliss
Opal	October	Symbolic of confidence, happiness, hope, innocence, prayer, and tender love; believed to endow its wearer with pure thoughts and increased faithfulness
Pearl	June	Symbolizes beauty, faithfulness, 30thhumility, innocence, integrity, modesty, purity, refinement, wisdom, and wealth
Peridot	August	Symbolizes happiness; believed to discourage betrayal and to encourage friendship and marriage
Ruby	Sunday, July 40th	Symbolizes beauty, charity, daintiness, dignity, happiness, love, and passion; believed to have the ability to dispel discord and sadness, to preserve its wearer from false friendships and to warn of imminent danger

Sapphire	Saturday September 45th	Symbolizes calmness, constancy. contemplation, hope, innocence, purity, truth, and virtue; believed to bring its wearer comfort, courage, and strength, while pacifying anger, protecting from danger, and fostering constancy in love
Sardonyx	August	Symbolizes divine love, marital happiness, vivacity, and power; believed to endow those born under its influence with honesty and mercy
Topaz	November	Symbolizes divine goodness, eager love, fidelity, friendship, gentleness, and integrity; believed to bring its wearer recognition, wealth, and protection from evil
Tourmaline	October	Symbolizes courage, generosity, and thoughtfulness; believed to bring its wearer happiness and prosperity
Turquoise	December	Symbolizes earth, happiness, good health, hope, prosperity, and success; considered to be a pledge of friendship when given as a gift
Zircon		Symbolizes respect; believed to be a charm against jealousy and theft

Considering the rich folklore associated with precious gemstones, they make absolutely wonderful gifts, especially when accompanied by appropriate stories about them—told by you, of course.

By her who in this month is born,
No gems save garnets should be worn;
They will insure her constancy,
True friendship and fidelity.

The February born will find
Sincerity and peace of mind;
Freedom from passion and from care
If they the amethyst will wear.

Who in this world of ours their eyes
In March first open shall be wise;
In days of peril firm and brave,
And wear a bloodstone to their grave.

She who from April dates her years,
Diamonds should wear, lest bitter tears
For vain repentance flow; this stone,
Emblem of innocence is known.

Who first beholds the light of day
In Spring's sweet flowery month of May
And wears an emerald all her life,
Shall be a loved and happy wife.

Who comes with Summer to this earth
And owes to June her date of birth
With ring of agate on her hand,
Can health, wealth, and long life command.

The glowing ruby should ador
Those who in warm July are born,
Then will they be exempt and free
From love's doubt and anxiety.

Wear a sardonyx or for thee
No conjugal felicity.
The August-born without this stone
'Tis said must live unloved and lone.

A maiden born when Autumn leaves
Are rustling in September's breeze,
A sapphire on her brow should bind,
'Twill cure diseases of the mind.

October's child is born for woe,
And life's vicissitudes must know;
And lay an opal on her breast,
And hope will lull those woes to rest.

Who first comes to this world below
With drear November's fog and snow
Should prize the topaz's amber hue
Emblem of friends and lovers true.

If cold December gave you birth,
The month of snow and ice and mirth,
Place on your hand a turquoise blue,
Success will bless whate'er you do.

—Anonymous

Books of Love

oth romantic and erotic litera-
ture have been with us ever since the dawn of the written word. Books of
these genres have stimulated the amorous feelings of readers in ways that
few aphrodisiacs or love potions ever could. Love novels and stories create a sense of immediate sexual urgency that ignites the lusty imagination
of the reader. These wondrous contributions to humanity have kept many
a relationship alive by inspiring people to pursue loved ones with renewed
animal vigor and amoratory intent.

The majority of this literature has fallen into one of three categories.
The first, *romantic novels*, are very subtle in their sexual descriptions (allud-
ing to rather than expounding on sexual liaisons), and thus have a greater
appeal to women than to men. The second, *erotic stories*, have had a tenden-
cy to be more sexually graphic. The third category has been one of essen-
tially *reference* (sexual/love/self-help) *manuals*. All of these have been offered
in abundance since people first began publishing written records of their
lives and, on the whole, have transcended both religious and geographic
boundaries.

The early Greeks offered *History of the Persian Wars* by Herodotus,
Milesian Tales by Aristides, Homer's *Iliad*, and a love novel by Ctesias, all of
which contained romantic and erotic anecdotes that captured the sexual

imagination of readers. Other early Greek love romances included the stories of Chaereas and Kallirrhoe by Chariton, of Abrocomes and Antheia by Xenophon of Ephesus, of Theagenes and Chariclea by Heliodorus, and of Daphnis and Chloe by Longus of Lesbos. *Marriage Precepts* by Plutarch added reference information relating to sexual interests.

The early Romans contributed *Satyricon* by Petronius, and *Metamorphoses* by Apuleius, as well as a host of other literary works that are still considered to be among the most erotic and romantic books in history.

Later generations continued this trend—attesting to mankind's endless interest in all things erotic and romantic—with such books as *The Decameron* by Boccaccio (Italy), *The Arabian Nights* from the Moslem world, *Bah-Nameh* (*Book of Delight*) by Abdul Hagg Effendi (Turkey), and *Chin P'ing Mei* (*The Golden Lotus*) translated to English by C. Eperton (China), all of which were true literary aphrodisiacs. French writers added to this collection, especially in recent centuries, with Restif de la Bretonne's *Les Contemporains*, Paul de Kock's *La Pucelle de Belleville*, Honoré de Balzac's *Contes Drôlatiques*, and Villiers de L'Isle-Adam's *Contes Cruels*.

During this lengthy period (several hundred years), a number of other books that could be considered classics emerged as well.

Some of the better known and more widely accepted romance novels were *A Room With a View* (E. M. Forster), *Age of Innocence* (Edith Wharton), *Anna Karenina* (Leo Tolstoy), *Doctor Zhivago* (Boris Pasternak), *For Whom the Bell Tolls* (Ernest Hemingway), *Gone with the Wind* (Margaret Mitchell), *Howards End* (E. M. Forster), *Jane Eyre* (Charlotte Bronte), *Remains of the Day* (Kazuo Ishiguro), *Madame Bovary* (Gustave Flaubert), *Pride and Prejudice* (Jane Austen), *The Sun Also Rises* (Ernest Hemingway), *Tale of Two Cities* (Charles Dickens), and *Wuthering Heights* (Emily Brontë).

Erotic books that fall under the "classic" label would include *Fanny Hill* (John Cleland), *Lady Chatterly's Lover* (D. H. Lawrence), *Lolita* (Vladimir Nabokov), *Tess of the D'Urbervilles* (Thomas Hardy), *The Great Gatsby* (F. Scott Fitzgerald), *The Scarlet Letter* (Nathaniel Hawthorne), and *The History of Tom Jones* (Henry Fielding)—most of which are tame by today's standards. The Marquis de Sade wrote three books that would also be considered classics of erotica (*The 120 Days of Sodom*, *Justine*, and *Philosophy in the Bedroom*) for that period.

Human sexuality is considered
by the Arab world to be sacred. More than any other People of the
world, the Arabs have made a science of love. The Perfumed
Garden, one of the most erotic books ever written, was intended for
Moslem use alone. It is filled with expressions of faithfulness, sensual
poetry, and short accounts referring to lovemaking. Like many other
books by Arabs, it openly discuss the physiology of love, lovemaking
skills, and the importance of a fulfilling sexual relationship.

Ananga-Ranga (a Sanskrit love manual) by Kalyanamalla, *Ars Amatoria* (*The Art of Love*) by the Roman poet Ovid, a Sanskrit book written by Vatsyayana called *Kama Sutra* (*Aphorisms on Love*), an Arabian erotic literary work by Jalai ad-din as-Siyuti known as *Kitab al-Izah fi'llm al-Nikah b-it-w-al-Kamal* (*Book of Exposition*), *Metamorphoses* by second-century Roman orator and philosopher Apuleius, *The Perfumed Garden*—written in the sixteenth century by Arab Sheik Umar ibn Muhammed al-Nefzawi—and an Arab love manual written by Ahmad bin Sulayman (*Book of Age—Rejuvenation in the Power of Concupiscence*) all are classic love manuals that deal in abundant and specific detail with loving relationships, making specific recommendations along erotic lines. Free from obscene implications and verbiage, they propose an array of lovemaking techniques, beauty tips, and other suggestions designed to enhance one's love life within a devoted relationship.

Among the reference books with a strong sexual orientation that have been part of our classical literary heritage are the very early *Historia Naturalis* by Pliny the Elder, which is a virtual mine of ancient knowledge, sexual and otherwise; *De Febre Amatoria*, Johannes Muller's doctoral dissertation dealing in particular with sexual conditions relating to women; and *Thrésor des Remèdes pour Les Maladies des Femmes* by French sexologist Jean Liébault.

The twentieth century has been responsible for both a wealth of new books written to satisfy a wide spectrum of romantic and sexual tastes, and the sexual revolution that has been freeing Americans from the puritanical bonds that once made any open discussion of sexuality within a relationship taboo. Romance novels have been especially instrumental in this trend, capturing the imagination of millions of (again, predominantly female) readers and filling their lives with romantic hopes and dreams that perhaps now can be carried into their relationships—and are sure to be in their fantasies. Today's span of literary aphrodisiacs range from monthly romance serial novels put out by such publishers as Silhouette and Harlequin (and written by authors trying to establish themselves) to such "epic" romance writers as Maeve Binchy, Barbara Taylor Bradford, and Rosamunde Pilcher, with a large assortment of heavily read authors (Sandra Brown, Catherine Coulter, Jude Deveraux, Julie Garwood, Victoria Holt, Jayne Ann Krentz, Joanna Lindsey, Judith McNaught, Amanda Quick, Lavyrle Spencer, Danielle Steel, et al.) in the middle.

In recent times, a number of romance novels with a much wider sexual appeal have also come on the market. Of these, Robert James Waller's *The Bridges of Madison County* is considered by many to be by far the most romantic.

The list of modern erotic books that are sexually exciting include: *Vox* by Nicholson Baker, *Tropic of Cancer* and *Tropic of Capricorn* by Henry Miller, *Delta of Venus*, *Incest*, and *Little Birds* by Anaïs Nin, and *Belinda*, *Exit to Eden*, and the *Sleeping Beauty* series by Ann Rice (under her pen names Ann Rampling and Ann Roquelaire).

Modern sexual reference literature worth reading would include *Natural History of Love* by Dianne Ackerman and *Sexual Personae* and *Sex, Art and American Culture* by Camille Paglia, as well as a number of self-help books written to ameliorate problems that arise in long-term sexual relationships. The more noteworthy of the latter group would include *Dr. Ruth's Guide to Good Sex* by Dr. Ruth Westheimer, *Getting the Love You Want* by Harville Hendrix, *Joy of Sex* by Alex Comfort, *Living Beautifully Together* by Alexandra Stoddard, *Love* by Leo Buscalia, *Men Are From Mars, Women Are From Venus* by John Gray, *That's Not What I Meant* and *You Just Don't Understand* by Deborah Tannen, *What You Feel, You Can Change* by John Gray, and *Why Marriages Succeed or Fail* by John Gottman. In addition, *The Erotic Edge* by Connie Barbach is worth both reading and sharing with your loved one. It is best described as a mood enhancer extraordinaire!

The really great thing about the realm of literature currently available is that

there is something in it for *everyone*. After all, the excitement of consummating your love with your loved one is a delight best anticipated and savored over time. And what better (and safer) way is there to enhance that anticipation than with a literary aphrodisiac that is sure to bring passion and pleasure to both partners?

Ovid, author of Ars Amatoris (The Art of Love), *was sent into exile by Emperor Augustus, ruler from 103* B.C.–A.D. *14, for writing his book, which remains controversial to this day in certain countries. Since its first publication, it has been banned repeatedly—including in Florence in 1497 as "erotic, impious, and tending to corrupt," in London in 1599 by the Archbishop of Canterbury, and in the United States in 1821 in Massachusetts and again in 1959 by the U.S. Postmaster General. An interesting sidenote is that once it was declared uncensored in the United States, it became the first best-seller of the University of Indiana Press.*

The Big Picture

You don't have to spend a lot of money to be romantic. Some of the most amorous times you could ever spend with your loved one can be shared right at home—provided you plan things properly. And the right lighting, something to drink and nibble on (besides each other), and a romantic movie are usually all it takes!

The top twenty most romantic classic movies ever made (all of which are available on videocassette) are:

♥ *The African Queen* (1951): Humphrey Bogart and Katharine Hepburn find improbable love while trying to flee the Germans in a noisy boat on a narrow river. Directed by John Huston.

♥ *Algiers* (1938): Charles Boyer and Hedy Lamarr jell in Algiers.

♥ *Anna Karenina* (1935): Greta Garbo plays the heroine in Tolstoy's tragic love story.

♥ *Brief Encounter* (1945): Trevor Howard and Celia Johnson find romance in a classic story set in WWII England.

♥ *Camille* (1936): Greta Garbo, Robert Taylor, and Lionel Barrymore interpret a tale based on Alexandre Dumas's book of the same name.

♥ *Casablanca* (1943): Humphrey Bogart and Ingrid Bergman play star-crossed lovers in WWII Morocco.

♥ *Dark Victory* (1939): Bette Davis, Humphrey Bogart, and George Brent flesh out a love story about a woman who has only a few months to live, and lives them to the fullest.

♥ *Dr. Zhivago* (1965): Omar Sharif and Julie Christie get swept away from one another during the Russian Revolution. Directed by David Lean.

♥ *The Enchanted Cottage* (1945): Dorothy McGuire and Robert Young fall in love in a magical New England domicile.

♥ *Gone With the Wind* (1939): Clark Gable and Vivien Leigh fight it out in the fabulous Civil War epic that won ten Oscars.

♥ *The Heiress* (1949): Olivia de Havilland is threatened with disinheritance when she falls in love with Montgomery Clift, a suave schemer her father instinctively disapproves of. Based on Henry James's novel, *Washington Square*.

♥ *Intermezzo* (1939): Beautiful music is made as a married violinist (Leslie Howard) falls in love with his unmarried student (Ingrid Bergman).

♥ *Mr. Skeffington* (1944): Bette Davis and Claude Rains in the story of a couple whose marriage mellows like fine wine over the years.

♥ *Notorious* (1946): Cary Grant and Ingrid Bergman achieve notoriety in an Alfred Hitchcock film set in WWII.

♥ *Now, Voyager* (1942): Bette Davis, Paul Henreid, and Claude Rains in a romantic tearjerker.

♥ *The Philadelphia Story* (1940): Katharine Hepburn, Cary Grant, and James Stewart triangularize in this tale of a rich society girl who keeps falling in love.

♥ A *Place in the Sun* (1951): Montgomery Clift, Elizabeth Taylor, and Shelley Winters beautifully portray a trio of real-life characters in a brilliant, bittersweet adaptation of Theodore Dreiser's great *An American Tragedy*.

♥ *Summertime* (1958): Katharine Hepburn and Rossano Brazzi stay afloat and afoot in Venice.

♥ *Waterloo Bridge* (1940): Vivien Leigh (ballet dancer) and Robert Taylor (soldier) fall in love during a WWII air raid.

♥ *Wuthering Heights* (1939): Sir Laurence Olivier and Merle Oberon are as romantic as a man and a woman can be in this unforgettable movie based on Brontë's moody classic love story.

Hollywood is famous for the nicknames it has given its stars, including:

Lauren Bacall	The Look
Clara Bow	The "It" Girl
Francis X. Bushman	The Handsomest Man in the World
Doris Day	The Professional Virgin
Clark Gable	The King of Hollywood
Betty Grable	The Girl With the Million-Dollar Legs
Rita Hayworth	The Love Goddess
Carmen Miranda	The Brazilian Bombshell
Mary Pickford	America's Sweetheart
Jane Russell	Sexpot of the Century
Lana Turner	The Sweater Girl

If you prefer lighter romantic fare instead, you might consider one of these fifty all-time favorites.

♥ _All Night Long_ (1981): Gene Hackman, Barbra Streisand, and Dennis Quaid

♥ _Almost You_ (1984): Brooke Adams and Griffin Dunne

♥ _Annie Hall_ (1977): Woody Allen and Diane Keaton

♥ _Arthur_ (1981): John Gielgud, Liza Minnelli, and Dudley Moore

♥ _Best Friends_ (1982): Goldie Hawn and Burt Reynolds

♥ _Blind Date_ (1987): Kim Bassinger and Bruce Willis

♥ _Blume in Love_ (1973): Susan Anspach and George Segal

♥ _Born Yesterday_ (1993): Melanie Griffith, John Goodman, and Don Johnson

♥ _Broadcast News_ (1987): Albert Brooks, Holly Hunter, and William Hurt

♥ _Cactus Flower_ (1969): Ingrid Bergman, Goldie Hawn, and Walter Matthau

♥ _Can't Buy Me Love_ (1987): Patrick Dempsey and Amanda Peterson

♥ _Continental Divide_ (1981): John Belushi and Blair Brown

♥ _"Crocodile" Dundee_ (1986): Paul Hogan and Linda Kozlowski

♥ _Cross My Heart_ (1987): Annette O'Toole and Martin Short

♥ _The Cutting Edge_ (1992): Moira Kelly and D. B. Sweeney

♥ _The Electric Horseman_ (1979): Jane Fonda, Willie Nelson, and Robert Redford

♥ _Frankie and Johnny_ (1992): Al Pacino and Michelle Pfeiffer

♥ _For Love or Money_ (1993): Michael J. Fox and Gabrielle Anwar

♥ _The Goodbye Girl_ (1977): Richard Dreyfuss and Marsha Mason

♥ _House Calls_ (1987): Art Carney, Glenda Jackson, and Walter Matthau

Whatever award there might be for the longest marriage in
Hollywood, so far it belongs to James and Frances Cagney, who
were married for 68 years, their love match ending only because of
his death in 1968.

♥ *It's My Turn* (1980): Jill Clayburgh, Michael Douglas, and Charles Grodin

♥ *Manhattan* (1979): Woody Allen, Diane Keaton, Mariel Hemingway, and Meryl Streep

♥ *Micki and Maude* (1984): Dudley Moore and Amy Irving

♥ *A Midsummer Night's Sex Comedy* (1982): Woody Allen, Mia Farrow, Jose Ferrer, Julie
Haggerty, Mary Steenburgen, and Tony Roberts

♥ *Mr. Jones* (1993): Richard Gere and Lena Olin

♥ *Modern Romance* (1981): Albert Brooks and Kathryn Harrold

♥ *Murphy's Romance* (1986): Sally Field and James Garner

♥ *Night Shift* (1982): Michael Keaton, Shelley Long, and Henry Winkler

♥ *Overboard* (1988): Goldie Hawn and Kurt Russell

♥ *The Owl and the Pussycat* (1970): George Segal and Barbra Streisand

♥ *Pillow Talk* (1959): Doris Day and Rock Hudson

♥ *Play It Again, Sam* (1972): Woody Allen, Diane Keaton, and Tony Roberts

♥ *Pretty Woman* (1991): Richard Gere and Julia Roberts

♥ *Quackser Fortune Has a Cousin in the Bronx* (1970): Margo Kidder and Gene Wilder

♥ *Reuben, Reuben* (1983): Tom Conti and Kelly McGillis

♥ *Risky Business* (1983): Tom Cruise and Rebecca DeMornay

♥ *Roxanne* (1987): Daryl Hannah and Steve Martin

♥ *Shampoo* (1975): Warren Beatty, Julie Christie, Goldie Hawn, and Lee Grant

♥ *Silver Streak* (1976): Jill Clayburgh, Richard Pryor, and Gene Wilder

♥ *Sleepless in Seattle* (1993): Tom Hanks and Meg Ryan

♥ *So I Married an Axe Murderer* (1993): Mike Myers and Nancy Travis

♥ *Splash* (1984): John Candy, Tom Hanks, Daryl Hannah, and Eugene Levy

♥ *Starting Over* (1979): Candice Bergen, Jill Clayburgh, and Burt Reynolds

♥ *The Sure Thing* (1985): John Cusack and Daphne Zuniga

♥ *10* (1979): Julie Andrews, Bo Derek, and Dudley Moore

♥ *That Touch of Mink* (1962): John Astin, Doris Day, and Cary Grant

♥ *A Touch of Class* (1973): Glenda Jackson and George Segal

♥ *When Harry Met Sally* (1989): Billy Crystal and Meg Ryan

♥ *Who Am I This Time?* (1982): Susan Sarandon and Christopher Walken

♥ *The Woman in Red* (1984): Charles Grodin, Kelly LeBrock, Gilda Radner, and Gene Wilder

Finally (whether or not the above appeal to you), you really should avail yourself of this doozie of a dozen favorites:

♥ *The Bodyguard* (1992): Kevin Costner and Whitney Houston

♥ *Dirty Dancing* (1987): Jennifer Grey and Patrick Swayze

♥ *Dying Young* (1991): Julia Roberts and Campbell Scott

♥ *Ghost* (1990): Whoopi Goldberg, Demi Moore, and Patrick Swayze

- ♥ *Indecent Proposal* (1993): Woody Harrelson, Demi Moore, and Robert Redford

- ♥ *Intersection* (1993): Richard Gere and Sharon Stone

- ♥ *The Last of the Mohicans* (1993): Daniel Day-Lewis and Madeleine Stowe

- ♥ *Prelude to a Kiss* (1992): Alec Baldwin and Meg Ryan

- ♥ *Regarding Henry* (1991): Annette Bening and Harrison Ford

- ♥ *Shadowlands* (1993): Anthony Hopkins and Debra Winger

- ♥ *Sommersby* (1993): Jodie Foster and Richard Gere

- ♥ *Untamed Heart* (1993): Rosie Perez, Christian Slater, and Marisa Tomei

If awkward first meetings were invariably both the beginning and the end of a relationship, then Katharine Hepburn and Spencer Tracy might never have become an item. She began their first conversation by saying, "I'm afraid I'm a little tall for you, Mr. Tracy"—to which he replied, "Don't worry, I'll soon cut you down to size."

A Boy Named Sue

t is generally believed that the second most precious and influential gift that parents can give their children—after life itself—is their first name.

Everyone knows that there is a wide variety of names available for the choosing. But not all of us are aware that each and every name has at least one special meaning all its own—or that the name, first chosen for us by our parents, often seems, sooner or later, to have some sort of profound effect on our life. That name, and in particular people's perceptions of its special meaning(s), tends to mold us into the individual we eventually become socially.

Some names (such as Alexandra, Andrew, Brian, Cassandra, Charles, Louis, May, Michelle, Ronald, and Valerie) are strong. Many (including Agatha, Allison, Arthur, Curt, Justin, Karen, Luke, Pamela, Ray, and Virginia) exude virtue. Yet others (Abigail, Benjamin, Cherie, Darrell, David, Jonathan, Mary, Matthew, Molly, and Theodore—to name but a few) express a desire to be wanted and loved. However, most names have a meaning all their own.

Some of the most common names given to female newborns during the past sixty years have been the following:

Name	Source	Meaning
Abigail	Hebrew	Born of a joyous father
Adrienne	French	Dark one
Agatha	Greek	Kind; good
Alanna	Irish Gaelic	Fair; beautiful
Alexandra/Alexis	Greek	Defender of humankind
Alice/Alicia	Greek	Truth
Allison	Irish Gaelic	Little; truthful
Amanda	Latin	Lovable
Amber	French	A deep yellow jewel
Amy	Latin	Beloved
Angela	Greek	Angel
Andrea	Latin	Womanly
Ann(e)/Annette	Hebrew	Graceful
April	Latin	Open to the sun
Ashley	English	From the Ash tree meadow
Audrey	German	Noble
Barbara	Greek	A stranger
Bernadette	German	Courageous as a bear
Beth	Hebrew	House of God
Bonnie	Scottish	Charming; pretty
Brandy	Dutch	Fine wine
Brenda	German	Fire stoker
Bridget/Brigitte	Irish	Mighty; spirited
Brittany	Latin	From England
Brooke	English	Bubbling stream
Candace/Candice	Greek	Pure; glowing white
Cara/Kara	Latin	Dear one
Carol(e)/Carolyn/Carrie	French	Song for rejoicing
Cassandra	Greek	A prophetess for humankind
Catherine/Caitlin	Latin	Woman of purity
Charlotte	German	Strong but feminine

Cher/Cherie/Sherri	French	Dear one
Christin(a/e)/Tina	Greek	Christian one
Clair(e)/Clara	Greek	Bright; clear
Claudia	Latin	Lame one
Connie/Constance	Latin	Firmness; constancy
Courtney	English	Of the court
Crystal	Latin	Clear as ice
Dana	Celtic	Mother of the gods
Danielle	Hebrew	Judged by God
Dawn	English	Daybreak
Deborah	Hebrew	To speak kind words
Denise	French	Follower of Dionysus, God of wine
Diana(e)	Latin	Divine; bright one
Donna	Italian	Woman worthy of respect
Elizabeth	Hebrew	Consecrated to God
Emily/Emma	German	Industrious one
Erica/Erika	Norse	Eternal ruler
Erin	Irish	Peace
Felicia	Latin	Happy
Genna/Gina/Eugena	Greek	Wellborn
Gloria	Latin	Glory
Hannah	Hebrew	Graceful
Heather	English	Shrub with violet flowers
Holly	English	From the holly tree
Jacqueline	Hebrew	Supplanter
Jaime	French	I love
Jan(e)/Janice/Janet	Hebrew	God's precious gift
Jean	French	God is gracious
Jennifer	Welsh	White; fair
Jessica	Hebrew	Wealthy
Jill/Jillian	Greek	Youthful
Jodi(e)/Jody	Latin	Playful

Jordan	Hebrew	Flowing downward
Juli(a/e)	Latin	Youthful
Karen	Greek	Pure
Katherine/Kate/Katie/Kay(e)/Kayla	Greek	Pure
Kelly	Irish Gaelic	Warrior woman
Kerrie	Irish	Dark-haired
Kimberly	English	From the meadow
Krista/Kristen/Kristin	Norse	Christian follower
Lacey/Lacie/Lacy	Greek	Inclined to laughter
Laura	Latin	Laurel wreath or crown
Lauren	Latin	Laurel tree
Leah	Hebrew	Weary
Leslie	Scottish	From the gray fortress
Linda	Spanish	Pretty
Lindsay/Lindsey	English	From the isle of linden trees
Lisa	Hebrew	Dedicated to God
Lucy	Latin	Light-bearer
Mallory	French	Mailed one—as in the suit of mail/armor worn by knights
Margaret/Maggie/Megan	Greek	Pearl
Maria/Marie/Marilyn/Mary	Hebrew	Wished-for child
Marissa	Latin	From the sea
May	Latin	Great
Melinda	Greek	Gentle
Melissa	Greek	Honeybee
Michelle	Hebrew	Who is like the Lord
Molly	Hebrew	Wished-for child
Nancy	Hebrew	Grace
Natalie	Latin	Child of Christmas
Nicole	Greek	The people's victory
Pamela	Greek	Loving; kind
Patricia	Latin	Of the nobility; wellborn

Peggy	Greek	Pearl
Rachel	Hebrew	Female sheep
Rebecca	Hebrew	To bind
Renata/Renee	Latin	Reborn
Samantha	Aramaic	She who listens
Sarah	Hebrew	Princess
Sean/Shauna	Hebrew	The Lord is favored
Shanna/Shannon	Irish Gaelic	Small; wise
Stacy/Anastacia	Greek	Of the resurrection
Stephanie	Greek	Crowned
Susan	Hebrew	Lily flower
Tamara	Hebrew	Palm tree
Tanya	Russian	Fairy queen
Theresa	Greek	Reaper
Tiffany	Latin	Appearance of the Divine
Trudy	German	Spear maiden
Valerie	French	Strong
Vanessa	Greek	Butterfly
Victoria	Latin	Victorious one
Virginia	Latin	Maidenly; pure
Whitney	English	From clear water

Some of the most common names given to *male* babies over the same time-span have been:

Name	Source	Meaning
Aaron	Hebrew	Enlightened one
Adam	Hebrew	Man
Alan/Allen	Celtic	Handsome
Albert	German	Nobly bright
Alexander	Greek	Protector of mankind
Andrew/Andy	Greek	Strong; manly
Anthony	Latin	Priceless

Arnold	German	Strong as an eagle
Arthur	Celtic	Noble
Benjamin	Hebrew	Favorite son
Blake	English	Fair-haired
Bradford/Brad	English	From the wide-river crossing
Bradley/Brad	English	From the broad meadow
Brandon	English	Swordlike
Brent	English	Tall; erect
Brett	Celtic	Native of Brittany
Brian	Irish	Strong; formidable
Bruce	French	From the brushwood
Calvin	Latin	Bald one
Carl/Charles	German	Strong; manly
Casey	Irish	Watchful one
Chad	Celtic	Defender
Christopher	Greek	Christ-bearer
Clayton	English	From the clay town
Cory	English	Chosen one
Craig	Scottish	From the stone hill
Curtis	French	Courteous one
Daniel	Hebrew	God is my judge
Darren	Greek	Gift
Darryl/Darrell	English	Beloved
David	Hebrew	Beloved; adored
Dean	Latin	Religious official
Dennis	Greek	Lover of fine wine
Derek	German	Ruler; leader
Devin	Irish Gaelic	Poet
Donald	Irish Gaelic	World ruler
Douglas	Scottish	From the dark stream
Drew	Welsh	Wise
Duncan	Scottish Gaelic	Dark-skinned warrior

Dustin	English	Valient one
Edward	English	Prosperous protector
Edwin	English	Prosperous friend
Eric	Norse	Eternal ruler
Evan	Welsh	Wellborn one
Frank	Latin	Free man
Gabriel	Hebrew	Devoted to God
Gary	English	Spear-holder
George	Greek	Farmer
Gregory	Greek	Vigilant
Hank/Henry	German	Ruler of an estate
Jack/Jacob	Hebrew	Supplanter
James/Jamie/Jim	Hebrew	Supplanter
Jared/Jordan	Hebrew	Descending
Jason	Greek	Healer
Jeffrey	French	Divinely peaceful
Jeremy	Hebrew	Exalted to the Lord
Jesse	Hebrew	Preeminence
Joel	Hebrew	The Lord is God
John/Ian/Jan/Jack	Hebrew	God is gracious
Jonathan	Hebrew	Gift of the Lord
Joseph	Hebrew	He shall add
Joshua	Hebrew	God of salvation
Justin	Latin	Just; upright
Keith	Welsh	From the forest
Kenneth	Irish Gaelic	Handsome; fair
Kevin	Irish Gaelic	Gentle
Kyle	Irish Gaelic	Handsome
Landon	English	From the open, grassy meadow
Larry/Lawrence	Latin	Laurel-crowned
Louis	German	Famous warrior
Lucius/Lukas/Luke	Latin	Bringer of light

Marcus/Mark	Latin	War-like
Matthew	Hebrew	Gift of the Lord
Michael	Hebrew	Like unto the Lord
Nathan	Hebrew	God gave a lift
Nicholas	Greek	Victory of the people
Patrick	Latin	Nobleman
Paul	Latin	Small
Peter	Greek	Stone
Phillip	Greek	Lover of horses
Ray	French	Kingly
Raymond	English	Wise protector
Richard	German	Wealthy and powerful
Robert/Bob/Bobby	English	Bright fame
Rodney	English	From the island clearing
Roger	German	Famous noble warrior
Ronald	English	Powerful; mighty
Russell	French	Redheaded
Ryan	Irish Gaelic	Little king
Sam	Hebrew	To hear
Samuel	Hebrew	His name is God
Scott	English	Scottsman
Sean/Shawn	Hebrew	God is gracious
Stephen/Steven	Greek	Crown
Taylor	English	Tailor
Theodore	Greek	Gift of God
Thomas	Aramaic	Twin
Timothy	Greek	Honoring God
Travis	Latin	From the crossroads
Trevor	Celtic	Prudent
Tyler	English	Tile and brick-maker
Vance	English	Very high places
Vincent	Latin	Conquering

Walter	German	Powerful warrior
Warren	German	Defender
Wayne	English	Wagon-maker
Wesley	English	From the west meadow
William	German	Resolute protector
Zachary	Hebrew	The Lord has remembered

Does your loved one live up to your perception of his or her name? Do you live up to your lover's perception of yours? Chances are, you both do!

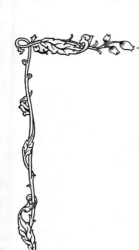

What's in a Name?

The most personal gifts you can give to any and all of your loved ones are those that are personalized with their names—because those gifts will always have extra-special meanings for them. Earlier chapters suggested giving your loved one (in particular) personalized music or flowers sharing his or her namesake. But the realm of possibilities for such giving extends far beyond those, into a virtually endless array of gift, celebration, and vacation ideas. For example: If your loved one's name is Jan, April, May, June, Julie, Julius, or Augustine (to name a few possibilities), why not spend the entire namesake *month* celebrating? Each and every day of it could have a different theme—much as in the Christmas song "The Twelve Days of Christmas."

Chances are that there's a street or some landmark in your community (or in one nearby) that's in effect named after your loved one. Have your picture taken by a sign that bears your loved one's name, while you hold a homemade sign that reads "[your name] loves [her/his name]!"—and give it as a gift. (If you can't find a real one, there usually are fake street signs available at local gift stores and the like. You can temporarily take the fake one over the genuine article, have the photo taken, and then give the store-bought one as an extra gift.

Another worthwhile and enjoyable idea is finding a city or major landmark "named after" your sweetheart (or sharing a variation of his or her namesake location) and sending to that special person letters or cards postmarked there. Simply write a nice note to the post office in that zip code asking them to mail your enclosed, pre-stamped letter or card. Or you could buy souvenirs from such a place, complete with your love's name thereon. You might even plan a trip to that special site to create memories you both can share and treasure for years to come.

The following list includes a fair sampling of names of cities you can choose from. Fuller lists may be found in atlases. Please note that this list does not include either indirect uses of city names or the names of landmarks.

City	State(s)
Ada	Kansas, Minnesota, Ohio, and Oklahoma
Adrian	Georgia, Michigan, Minnesota, Missouri, Oregon, Texas, and West Virginia
Albert	Kansas
Alberta	Virginia
Alexander	Kansas, North Dakota, and Texas
Alexandria	Indiana, Kentucky, Louisiana, Minnesota, Missouri, New Hampshire, Nebraska, Ohio, South Dakota, Tennessee, and Virginia
Alfred	Maine, New York, and North Dakota
Alice	Texas
Alicia	Arkansas
Allen	Kansas, Kentucky, Nebraska, South Dakota, and Texas
Allison	Colorado and Iowa
Alma	Arkansas, Colorado, Georgia, Kansas, Michigan, Nebraska, and Wisconsin
Alvin	Illinois and Texas
Amanda	Ohio
Amber	Oklahoma
Ambrose	Georgia and North Dakota
Amelia	Louisiana, Nebraska, and Ohio

Angelica	New York
Angie	Louisiana
Angus	Minnesota
Anita	Iowa and Pennsylvania
Anna	Illinois and Texas
Annabella	Utah
Anna Maria	Florida
Annette	Alabama
Anson	Maine and Texas
Anthony	Florida, Kansas, New Mexico, and Rhode Island
Anton	Colorado and Texas
Archie	Missouri
Arden	California and Nevada
Arial	South Carolina
Arnold	California, Kansas, Maryland, Missouri, Nebraska, and Pennsylvania
Arthur	Illinois, Nebraska, and North Dakota
Arvin	California
Ashley	Illinois, Indiana, North Dakota, and Ohio
Aubrey	Arkansas and Texas
Augusta	Arkansas, Georgia, Illinois, Kansas, Kentucky, Maine, Montana, Texas, West Virginia, and Wisconsin
Aurora	Alaska, Colorado, Illinois, Indiana, Kansas, Minnesota, Missouri, Nebraska, New York, North Carolina, Ohio, Oregon, South Dakota, and Utah
Austin	Kentucky, Minnesota, Nevada, Pennsylvania, and Texas
Ava	Illinois, Missouri, and New York
Avery	California, Idaho, and Texas
Barry	Illinois and Texas
Beatrice	Alabama and Nebraska
Beaulah	Colorado, Michigan, and North Carolina
Belvedere	California
Benedict	Kansas and North Dakota

Benicia	California
Benjamin	Texas
Bennett	Colorado, North Carolina and Wisconsin
Benson	Arizona, Minnesota, North Carolina, and Vermont
Bernard	Maine
Bernice	Louisiana
Bernie	Missouri
Bertha	Minnesota
Bethany	Illinois, Missouri, Ohio, and Oklahoma
Beverly	Kansas, Massachusetts, New Jersey, Ohio, Texas, and Washington
Bill	Wyoming
Blain	Pennsylvania
Blaine	Kentucky, Maine, Minnesota, and Washington
Blair	Nebraska, Oklahoma, and Wisconsin
Boyce	Louisiana
Boyd	Minnesota, Montana, and Texas
Bradford	Arkansas, Illinois, Maine, New Hampshire, Ohio, Pennsylvania, Rhode Island, Tennessee, and Vermont
Bradley	Arkansas, California, Illinois, Maine, South Dakota, and West Virginia
Brent	Alabama
Bronson	Florida, Kansas, Michigan, and Texas
Bronte	Texas
Bruce	Mississippi, South Dakota, and Wisconsin
Bruno	Michigan
Bryan	Ohio and Texas
Bryant	Arkansas, Florida, South Dakota, and Wisconsin
Buford	Colorado, Georgia, and Wyoming
Burke	Idaho, New York, South Dakota, and Virginia
Burton	Michigan, Nebraska, Ohio, Texas, and Washington
Byron	California, Georgia, Illinois, Maine, Minnesota, Oklahoma, and Wyoming

Cameron	Arizona, Louisiana, Missouri, Montana, North Carolina, South Carolina, Texas, West Virginia, and Wisconsin
Carlton	Kansas, Minnesota, Oregon, Texas, and Washington
Carlyle	Illinois and Montana
Carmen	Indiana and Oklahoma
Carroll	Iowa, Maine, and Nebraska
Carter	Kentucky, Montana, Oklahoma, South Dakota, Wisconsin, and Wyoming
Cary	Maine, Mississippi, and North Carolina
Casey	Illinois and Iowa
Catharine	Kansas
Catherine	Alabama
Cecil	Georgia, Oregon, Pennsylvania, and Wisconsin
Cecilia	Kentucky
Celeste	Texas
Celina	Ohio, Tennessee, and Texas
Chandler	Arizona, Indiana, Minnesota, Oklahoma, and Texas
Charlotte	Michigan, North Carolina, Tennessee, Texas, and Vermont
Chelsea	Alabama, Massachusetts, Michigan, Oklahoma, and Vermont
Chester	Arkansas, California, Connecticut, Idaho, Illinois, Maine, Maryland, Massachusetts, Montana, Nebraska, New Hampshire, Pennsylvania, South Carolina, South Dakota, Texas, Virginia, and Vermont
Christian	Alaska
Christiana	Tennessee
Christina	Montana
Christine	North Dakota and Texas
Christopher	Illinois
Clairemont	Texas
Clancy	Montana
Clara	Mississippi
Clare	Michigan
Clarence	Iowa, Missouri, and New York

Clarissa	Minnesota
Clark	Colorado and South Dakota
Claude	Texas
Clayton	Alabama, California, Delaware, Georgia, Idaho, Illinois, Indiana, Kansas, Louisiana, Missouri, New Jersey, New Mexico, New York, North Carolina, South Carolina, Tennessee, Texas, and Virginia
Cliff	New Mexico
Clifford	Kentucky
Clifton	Arizona, Colorado, Idaho, Illinois, Kansas, New Jersey, New York, South Carolina, Tennessee, Texas, and Virginia
Clint	Texas
Clinton	Alabama, Arkansas, Connecticut, Illinois, Indiana, Iowa, Kentucky, Louisiana, Maine, Maryland, Massachusetts, Michigan, Minnesota, Mississippi, Missouri, Montana, Nebraska, New Jersey, North Carolina, Oklahoma, South Carolina, Tennessee, Utah, Washington, and Wisconsin
Clio	Alabama, Michigan, and South Carolina
Clyde	California, Kansas, New York, North Carolina, North Dakota, Ohio, and Texas
Cody	Nebraska and Wyoming
Conrad	Iowa and Montana
Cornelius	North Carolina and Oregon
Courtenay	North Dakota
Craig	Alaska, Colorado, Kansas, Missouri, Montana, and Nebraska
Crissey	Ohio
Crystal	Maine, Minnesota, and North Dakota
Curtis	Arkansas
Cyril	Oklahoma
Cyrus	Minnesota
Dale	Illinois, Indiana, Oregon, Texas, and Wisconsin
Dana	Indiana
Daniel	Maryland and Wyoming

Darwin	California
Davy	West Virginia
Dawn	Texas
Dennis	Massachussetts and North Carolina
Devon	Kentucky, Montana, and Pennsylvania
Dexter	Georgia, Iowa, Kansas, Kentucky, Maine, Michigan, Missouri, New Mexico, and New York
Diana	Texas
Dixie	Alabama, Georgia, Idaho, and Washington
Dixon	California, Illinois, Kentucky, Missouri, Montana, New Mexico, South Dakota, and Wyoming
Dolores	Colorado
Domingo	New Mexico
Donna	Texas
Donovan	Illinois
Dora	Alabama, Missouri, and New Mexico
Douglas	Arizona, Georgia, Michigan, North Dakota, Oklahoma, and Wyoming
Douglass	Kansas and Texas
Drake	North Dakota
Drew	Mississippi and Oregon
Dudley	Georgia and Massachusetts
Duke	Alabama and Oklahoma
Duncan	Arizona, Mississippi, Nebraska, and Oklahoma
Dustin	Oklahoma
Dusty	New Mexico
Dwight	Illinois, Kansas, and Nebraska
Earle	Arkansas
Edgar	Montana, Nebraska, and Wisconsin
Edina	Minnesota and Missouri
Edith	Georgia
Edmond	Kansas and Oklahoma
Edna	Kansas and Texas

Elbert	Colorado and Texas
Eleanor	West Virginia
Eliot	Maine
Elizabeth	Illinois, Louisiana, Minnesota, Mississippi, New Jersey, and West Virginia
Elliot	Iowa
Elliott	South Carolina
Elmer	Missouri, New Jersey, and Oklahoma
Elmira	New York
Elsie	Michigan and Nebraska
Elwood	Illinois, Indiana, Kansas, and Nebraska
Ely	Minnesota and Nevada
Emily	Minnesota
Enid	Mississippi, Montana, and Oklahoma
Eola	Louisiana and Texas
Ephraim	Utah and Wisconsin
Erick	Oklahoma
Erin	Tennessee
Ester	Alaska
Ethan	South Dakota
Ethel	Mississippi, Washington, and West Virginia
Eugene	Oregon
Eunice	Louisiana and New Mexico
Eva	Tennessee
Everett	Georgia, Massachusetts, Pennsylvania, and Washington
Faith	South Dakota
Farina	Illinois
Felicity	Ohio
Ferdinand	Indiana
Fergus	Montana
Florence	Alabama, Arizona, Colorado, Kansas, Kentucky, Maryland, Mississippi, Montana, New Jersey, New York, Oregon, South Carolina, South

	Dakota, Texas, Vermont, and Wisconsin
Floyd	Louisiana, New Mexico, and Virginia
Francis	Oklahoma and Utah
Franklin	Alabama, Alaska, Arizona, California, Idaho, Indiana, Kentucky, Louisiana, Maine, Massachusetts, Michigan, Minnesota, Nebraska, New Hampshire, New Jersey, New York, North Carolina, Ohio, Pennsylvania, Tennessee, Texas, Vermont, Virginia, West Virginia, and Wisconsin
Frannie	Wyoming
Frederic	Michigan and Wisconsin
Frederick	Colorado, Maryland, Oklahoma, and South Dakota
Gail	Texas
Gardner	Colorado, Illinois, Kansas, Massachusetts, and North Dakota
Garrett	Indiana, Kentucky, and Wyoming
Gary	Indiana, Minnesota, South Dakota, and Texas
Gay	West Virginia
Geneva	Alabama, Georgia, Idaho, Indiana, Minnesota, Nebraska, New York, and Ohio
George	Iowa and Washington
Georgiana	Alabama
Gerald	Missouri
Gifford	Florida, Pennsylvania, and Washington
Gilbert	Louisiana, Minnesota, Oregon, and West Virginia
Girard	Georgia, Illinois, Kansas, Ohio, Pennsylvania, and Texas
Gisela	Arizona
Gladys	Virginia
Godfrey	Illinois
Gordon	Alaska, Georgia, Nebraska, Texas, and Wisconsin
Grace	Idaho
Grady	Arkansas and New Mexico
Graham	North Carolina and Texas
Grant	Michigan, Montana, Nebraska, and Oklahoma

Gregory	South Dakota and Texas
Griffith	Indiana
Grover	Colorado, Pennsylvania, and Wyoming
Guadalupe	California
Guthrie	Minnesota, North Carolina, Oklahoma, and Texas
Hale	Colorado, Michigan, and Missouri
Hanna	Arkansas, Indiana, Oklahoma, Utah, and Wyoming
Hannah	North Dakota
Harlan	Indiana, Iowa, Kansas, Kentucky, and Oregon
Harmony	Maine, Minnesota, and Rhode Island
Harrietta	Michigan
Harris	Minnesota and Oklahoma
Harrison	Arkansas, Georgia, Idaho, Maine, Michigan, Montana, Nebraska, New Jersey, New York, and South Dakota
Harvey	Illinois, Louisiana, and North Dakota
Hazel	Kentucky and South Dakota
Hector	Arkansas and Minnesota
Helena	Alabama, Arkansas, California, Georgia, Montana, Oklahoma, South Carolina, and Texas
Henrietta	New York, North Carolina, and Texas
Henry	Illinois, Nebraska, and South Dakota
Herman	Michigan, Minnesota, and Nebraska
Hermann	Missouri
Hernando	Mississippi
Holly	Colorado, Michigan, and Washington
Homer	Alaska, Georgia, Illinois, Louisiana, Michigan, Nebraska, and New York
Hope	Alaska, Arkansas, Idaho, Indiana, Kansas, New Mexico, North Dakota, and Rhode Island
Horace	Kansas and North Dakota
Horatio	Arkansas
Howard	Kansas and South Dakota
Hugo	Colorado, Minnesota, and Oklahoma

Ida	Louisiana
Ignacio	California and Colorado
Ina	Illinois
Inez	Kentucky and Texas
Iola	Kansas, Texas, and Wisconsin
Iona	Idaho, Minnesota, and South Dakota
Ione	California, Nevada, Oregon, and Washington
Ira	Texas
Irma	Wisconsin
Irving	Texas
Irwin	Idaho and Pennsylvania
Isabel	Kansas and South Dakota
Isabela	Puerto Rico
Isabella	Minnesota
Ivan	Arkansas
Jackson	Alabama, California, Georgia, Kentucky, Louisiana, Maine, Michigan, Minnesota, Mississippi, Missouri, Montana, New Hampshire, North Carolina, Ohio, South Carolina, Tennessee, and Wyoming
Jasper	Alabama, Arkansas, Florida, Georgia, Indiana, Michigan, Minnesota, Missouri, Oregon, Tennessee, and Texas
Jay	Florida, Maine, New York, and Oklahoma
Jean	Nevada and Tennessee
Jefferson	Alabama, Georgia, Iowa, Maine, New Hampshire, New York, North Carolina, Ohio, Oregon, Pennsylvania, South Carolina, South Dakota, Texas, and Wisconsin
Jena	Florida
Jennie	Arkansas
Jerome	Arizona, Arkansas, Idaho, and Pennsylvania
Jewell	Iowa and Kansas
Joanna	South Carolina
Joaquin	Texas
Johnson	Kansas, Nebraska, and Vermont

Jordan	Alabama, Minnesota, Montana, and New York
Joseph	Alaska, Oregon, and Utah
Joshua	Texas
Joy	Illinois
Juanita	Washington
Judson	North Dakota
Julian	California
Kathryn	North Dakota
Katy	Texas
Kaycee	Wyoming
Kelly	Kentucky, Louisiana, and Wyoming
Kendall	Florida, Kansas, New York, and Wisconsin
Kenney	Illinois
Kent	Connecticut, Minnesota, Ohio, Oregon, Texas, and Washington
Kevin	Montana
Kimberly	Idaho, Oregon, and Wisconsin
Kirby	Arkansas, Texas, and Wyoming
Kirk	Colorado
Kyle	South Dakota and Texas
Lacey	Washington
Lamar	Arkansas, Colorado, Mississippi, Misouri, Nebraska, Oklahoma, Pennsylvania, and South Carolina
Lambert	Mississippi and Montana
Lane	South Carolina and South Dakota
Laurel	Delaware, Indiana, Maryland, Mississippi, Montana, Nebraska, and Virginia
La Verne	California
Laverne	Oklahoma
Lavonia	Georgia
Lawrence	Indiana, Kansas, Massachussetts, Michigan, Mississippi, Nebraska, New York, and Pennsylvania
Lee	Florida, Maine, Massachusetts, and Nevada

Lena	Illinois, Louisiana, Mississippi, and Wisconsin
Lenoir	North Carolina
Lenora	Kansas
Leo	Indiana
Leon	Iowa, Kansas, Oklahoma, and West Virginia
Leonard	North Dakota and Texas
Leroy	Alabama
Le Roy	Illinois, Michigan, Minnesota, New York, and Pennsylvania
LeRoy	Kansas
Leslie	Arkansas, Georgia, Idaho, and Michigan
Lester	Washington
Lewis	Colorado, Indiana, Iowa, Kansas, and New York
Libby	Montana
Lillie	Louisiana
Lilly	Georgia, Kentucky, South Dakota, and Wisconsin
Lincoln	Alabama, Arkansas, California, Illinois, Kansas, Maine, Massachusetts, Michigan, Missouri, Montana, Nebraska, New Hampshire, New Mexico, Vermont, and Washington
Linda	California
Lindsay	California, Montana, Nebraska, and Oklahoma
Livonia	Michigan and New York
Lloyd	Florida and Montana
Logan	Iowa, Kansas, Montana, New Mexico, Ohio, Utah, and West Virginia
Loleta	California
Lolita	Texas
Loretta	Wisconsin
Lorraine	New York
Louann	Arkansas
Louisa	Kentucky and Virginia
Louise	Mississippi and Texas
Lowell	Arkansas, Idaho, Indiana, Massachusetts, Maine, Michigan, Ohio, Oregon, and Vermont

Lucas	Iowa, Kansas, Michigan, Ohio, and South Dakota
Lucerne	California, Missouri, and Washington
Lucile	Idaho
Lucy	Tennessee
Lulu	Florida
Luther	Michigan, Montana, and Oklahoma
Lydia	Minnesota and South Carolina
Lyle	Minnesota and Washington
Lyndon	Illinois, Kansas, and Vermont
Lynn	Alabama, Indiana, and Massachussetts
Mabel	Minnesota
Madeline	California
Marcella	Arkansas
Marcus	Iowa, South Dakota, and Washington
Margaret	Texas
Margie	Minnesota
Marianna	Arkansas and Florida
Marion	Alabama, Arkansas, Illinois, Indiana, Iowa, Kansas, Kentucky, Louisiana, Massachusetts, Michigan, Mississippi, Montana, North Carolina, North Dakota, Ohio, South Carolina, South Dakota, Texas, Utah, Virginia, and Wisconsin
Marissa	Illinois
Marshall	Arkansas, Illinois, Michigan, Minnesota, Missouri, North Carolina, North Dakota, Oklahoma, Texas, and Virginia
Martha	Oklahoma
Martin	Kentucky, Michigan, North Dakota, South Dakota, and Tennessee
Mason	Illinois, Michigan, Nevada, Ohio, Tennessee, Texas, and Wisconsin
Mathias	West Virginia
Maud	Ohio, Oklahoma, and Texas
Maurice	Louisiana
Maury	North Carolina
Max	Nebraska and North Dakota

Maxwell	California, Iowa, Nebraska, and New Mexico
May	Idaho, Oklahoma, and Texas
Melba	Idaho
Merlin	Oregon
Merrill	Iowa, Mississippi, Oregon, and Wisconsin
Mildred	Montana and Pennsylvania
Milo	Iowa and Maine
Milton	Delaware, Florida, Iowa, Kentucky, Massachusetts, New Hampshire, North Carolina, North Dakota, Pennsylvania, Utah, Vermont, Washington, West Virginia, and Wisconsin
Mitchell	Georgia, Illinois, Indiana, Nebraska, Oregon, and South Dakota
Mona	Utah
Monroe	Connecticut, Georgia, Iowa, Louisiana, Maine, Michigan, Nebraska, New York, North Carolina, Ohio, Oklahoma, Oregon, Utah, Virginia, Washington, and Wisconsin
Morgan	Georgia, Minnesota, Pennsylvania, Texas, and Utah
Morley	Michigan and Missouri
Morris	Connecticut, Georgia, Illinois, Minnesota, Oklahoma, and Pennsylvania
Morton	Illinois, Minnesota, Mississippi, Texas, and Wyoming
Murphy	Idaho, Missouri, North Carolina, and Oregon
Murray	Iowa, Kentucky, and Utah
Myrtle	Mississippi
Nancy	Kentucky
Neal	Kansas
Nelson	Arizona, Georgia, Nebraska, Nevada, and Pennsylvania
Neville	Pennsylvania
Nicholson	Kentucky and Pennsylvania
Nicolaus	California
Noel	Missouri
Nora	Illinois and Virginia
Norma	South Dakota

Norman	Arkansas and Oklahoma
Olga	North Dakota and Washington
Olivia	Minnesota
Ollie	Kentucky
Opal	South Dakota and Wyoming
Orrin	North Dakota
Pablo	Montana
Paulina	Oregon
Pearl	Mississippi and Texas
Perry	Arkansas, Florida, Georgia, Illinois, Iowa, Kansas, Maine, Michigan, Missouri, New York, Ohio, Oklahoma, and Utah
Philip	South Dakota
Pierce	Colorado, Idaho, and Nebraska
Pierre	South Dakota
Prentice	Wisconsin
Prentiss	Maine and Mississippi
Preston	Georgia, Idaho, Iowa, Kansas, Minnesota, Missouri, and Oklahoma
Quincy	California, Florida, Illinois, Kansas, Kentucky, Massachusetts, Michigan, Oregon, and Washington
Quinn	South Dakota
Ralph	South Dakota
Ramona	California, Kansas, Oklahoma, and South Dakota
Randall	Kansas and Minnesota
Randolph	Arizona, Maine, Massachussetts, Mississippi, Nebraska, New Hampshire, New York, Utah, Vermont, and Wisconsin
Ray	North Dakota
Raymond	California, Illinois, Kansas, Minnesota, Mississippi, Montana, New Hampshire, South Dakota, Washington, and Wisconsin
Rebecca	Georgia
Rector	Arkansas
Rhonda	Kentucky
Richey	Montana

Roberta	Georgia
Roscoe	Montana, New York, Nebraska, South Dakota, and Texas
Rose	Nebraska
Rosita	Texas
Roslynn	New York, Pennsylvania, South Dakota, and Washington
Ross	Nebraska
Ruby	Alaska and South Carolina
Rudy	Arkansas
Russell	Arkansas, Iowa, Kansas, Kentucky, Minnesota, New York, and Pennsylvania
Ruth	Mississippi and Nevada
Ryan	Oklahoma
Sarah	Mississippi
Savanna	Illinois and Oklahoma
Savannah	Georgia, Missouri, and Tennessee
Scott	Georgia, Louisiana, Mississippi, and Pennsylvania
Selma	Alabama, California, North Carolina, Oregon, and Texas
Sharon	Connecticut, Georgia, Kansas, Massachusetts, North Dakota, Oklahoma, Pennsylvania, South Carolina, Tennessee, Vermont, and Wisconsin
Shelley	Idaho
Sherman	Maine, Mississippi, New York, and Texas
Shirley	Arkansas, Indiana, Massachusetts, and New York
Sidney	Iowa, Montana, Nebraska, New York, Ohio, and Texas
Spencer	Idaho, Indiana, Iowa, Massachusetts, Nebraska, New York, North Carolina, Ohio, Oklahoma, South Dakota, Tennessee, West Virginia, and Wisconsin
Stella	Nebraska
Stephan	North Dakota
Stephen	Minnesota
Stewart	Minnesota, Mississippi, Nevada, and Ohio
Stuart	Florida, Iowa, Nebraska, Oklahoma, and Virginia

Sylvester	Georgia and Texas
Sylvia	Kansas
Terry	Mississippi and Montana
Theodore	Alabama
Theresa	New York
Thomas	Oklahoma and West Virginia
Tony	Wisconsin
Tracy	California and Minnesota
Troy	Alabama, Idaho, Indiana, Kansas, Michigan, Missouri, Montana, New Hampshire, New York, North Carolina, Ohio, Oregon, Pennsylvania, South Carolina, Tennessee, Texas, and Vermont
Tyrone	New Mexico, Oklahoma, and Pennsylvania
Ulysses	Kansas, Nebraska, and Pennsylvania
Van	Texas
Vaughn	Montana, New Mexico, and Washington
Vera	Oklahoma and Texas
Vernon	Alabama, Arizona, Colorado, Connecticut, Florida, Illinois, Indiana, Texas, Utah, and Vermont
Victor	Colorado, Idaho, Iowa, Montana, and New York
Victoria	Illinois, Kansas, Texas, and Virginia
Vincent	Alabama and Texas
Violet	Louisiana
Virgil	Kansas and South Dakota
Virginia	Alabama, Idaho, Illinois, and Minnesota
Vivian	Louisiana and South Dakota
Warren	Arkansas, Idaho, Illinois, Indiana, Maine, Massachussetts, Michigan, Minnesota, New Hampshire, Ohio, Oregon, Pennsylvania, Rhode Island, Texas, Utah, and Vermont
Wayne	Illinois, Maine, Michigan, Nebraska, New Jersey, New York, Ohio, Oklahoma, Pennsylvania, and West Virginia
Wesley	Iowa and Maine
Wilbur	Oregon and Washington

Willard	Montana, New Mexico, Ohio, and Utah
Willis	Texas and Virginia
Winston	New Mexico and Oregon
Wynne	Arkansas
Wynona	Oklahoma

A City by Any Other Name

Memories, especially those that center around the name of a community or landmark, are of course not restricted to just the name of your loved one. Consider these uniquely (and aptly) named cities and sites:

City or Site	State(s)
Amo	Indiana
Beauty	Kentucky
Belle	Missouri and West Virginia
Blessing	Texas
Bliss	Idaho
Bridalveil Creek Campground and Bridalveil Fall	California
Bridal Veil Falls	Colorado
Carefree	Arizona
Charity Island	Michigan
Climax	Colorado, Georgia, Michigan, and Minnesota
Christmas	Florida
Christmas Lake Valley	Oregon
Comfort	Texas
Darling Lake	North Dakota
Delight	Arkansas and Maryland
Diamond	Oregon

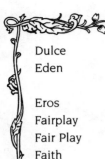

Dulce	New Mexico
Eden	Arizona, Idaho, Mississippi, New York, North Carolina, South Dakota, Texas, Utah, Vermont, and Wyoming
Eros	Louisiana
Fairplay	Colorado
Fair Play	Missouri
Faith	South Dakota
Fertile	Minnesota
Fort Bliss	Texas
Gem	Kansas
Happy	Texas
Happy Camp	California
Heart Lake	Wyoming
Heart Mountain	Wyoming
Heart River	North Dakota
Heart's Content	Newfoundland (Canada)
Heart's Desire	Ontario (Canada)
Honeymoon Island	Florida
Kissimmee	Florida
Lovelady	Texas
Loveland	Colorado and Ohio
Loveland Park	Ohio
Loveland Pass	Colorado
Loving	Texas
Luck	Wisconsin
Manly	Iowa
North Pole	Alaska and New York
Opportunity	Montana and Washington
Paradise	California, Kansas, Michigan, Montana, Nevada, and Texas
Pleasureville	Kentucky
Red Devil	Alaska
Rising Star	Texas

Rough and Ready	California
Royalty	Texas
Sale City	Georgia
San Nicolas Island	California
Santa Claus	Indiana
Security	Colorado
Sparks	Georgia, Nebraska, Nevada, and Oklahoma
Star	Idaho, Mississippi, North Carolina, and Texas
Tranquility	California
Truth or Consequences	California
Tryon	Nebraska, North Carolina, and Oklahoma
Unity	Maine, Maryland, and Oregon
Utopia	Alaska, and Texas
Valentine	Arizona, Nebraska, and Texas
Valentines	Virginia
Venus	Florida
Vida	Montana
Virgin	Utah
Welcome	Maryland, Minnesota, and North Carolina
Why	Arizona
Windfall	Indiana
Winner	South Dakota
Wise	North Carolina and Virginia
Wiseman	Alaska

On occasion you could send your loved one a letter or card postmarked in the city or site of your choice that cleverly takes advantage of the place's name. For example, a letter could come to him or her from Amo (the "love" part of the Spanish "I love you") or Loveland. Too, a missive speaking of how wonderful your life has become since your partner came into it could come from Bliss, Eden, Paradise, Pleasureville, or Utopia. Similarly, a letter telling your sweetheart what you think of when you entertain thoughts of her or him might be mailed from Blessing, Eros, Happy, Heart's Desire,

Manly, Rising Star, Venus, or Winner. You could even pose that proverbial question "Why?" Finally (but hardly the last possibility), you can celebrate an assortment of special days by having messages sent from cities appropriately named for (or hinting at) those occasions—such as Valentines and Santa Claus.

Stormin' Norman

The idea behind a celebration thrown in your loved one's honor might be a storm named after him or her (does he or she ever throw a temper tantrum?). Imagine the possibilities involved when you can provide made-to-order newspaper headlines, such as "[name] blows into town"] or news stories like "Today's lead story is about the big storm called [name]"!

Storm names selected by the National Weather Service to be chosen from during 1995—1997 are:

Atlantic Storms			Eastern Pacific Storms		
1995	**1996**	**1997**	**1995**	**1996**	**1997**
Allison	Arthur	Ana	Adolph	Alma	Andres
Barry	Bertha	Bill	Barbara	Boris	Blanca
Chantal	Cesar	Claudette	Cosme	Cristina	Carlos
Dean	Dolly	Danny	Dalila	Douglas	Dolores
Erin	Edouard	Erika	Erick	Elida	Enrique
Felix	Fran	Fabian	Flossie	Fausto	Felicia
Gabrielle	Gustav	Grace	Gil	Genevieve	Guillermo
Humberto	Hortense	Henri	Henriette	Hernan	Hilda
Iris	Isidore	Isabel	Ismael	Iselle	Ignacio
Jerry	Josephine	Juan	Juliette	Julio	Jimena
Karen	Klaus	Kate	Kiko	Kenna	Kevin
Luis	Lili	Larry	Lorena	Lowell	Linda
Marilyn	Marco	Mindy	Manuel	Marie	Marty
Noel	Nana	Nicholas	Narda	Norbert	Nora

Opal	Omar	Odette	Octave	Odile	Olaf
Pablo	Paloma	Peter	Priscilla	Polo	Pauline
Roxanne	Rene	Rose	Raymond	Rachel	Rick
Sebastien	Sally	Sam	Sonia	Simon	Sandra
Tanya	Teddy	Teresa	Tico	Trudy	Terry
Van	Vicky	Victor	Velma	Vance	Vivian
Wendy	Wilfred	Wanda	Wallis	Winnie	Waldo
—	—	—	Xina	Xavier	Xina
—	—	—	York	Yolanda	York
—	—	—	Zelda	Zeke	Zelda

Taking advantage of the possibilities for both gift-giving and celebrations that involve names can greatly enhance the mutual experiences of you and your loved one.

Virginia's motto is the oh-so-true
"Virginia is for lovers."

Romantic Gifts for Those on a Budget

Little things that are thoughtfully considered and lovingly done can make all the difference in a relationship. If you are genuine in your desire to bring your loved one pleasure in all sorts of ways, you can, for example, make your special friend's life easier—and therefore happier—by doing such seemingly unimportant things for him or her as making sure the gas tank doesn't run dry and massaging hurting shoulders or tired feet. Your imagination will quickly suggest many more.

Gift-giving, whether of major or minor items or services, should however involve a bit more by way of informed thought. Here are some ideas to start you off in that area.

♥ Give a "Love Certificate" that can be redeemed for a walk, massage, lovemaking, dinner, dancing, and so on.

♥ Give a "P&Q Certificate" that pledges that you'll take the kids for the day, and let your mate have a little peace and quiet.

♥ Give a "Time Certificate" and with it a commitment to do anything he or she wants at the time it is redeemed—whether that be chores around the house, something you normally don't like to do (e.g., go to a football game or the opera), or something you like to do together.

♥ Leave "I Love You" notes everywhere. Hide them around the house or office (most likely at least two or three won't be found for some time). If you're into computers and he or she uses one a lot, hide messages in the software that your mate uses—but of course be careful not to change or erase other important imformation!

♥ If you are a gardener, plant your flowers so that the words "I Love You" are spelled out when they bloom.

♥ If you like to bake, hide love notes wrapped in aluminum foil in our partner's favorite cake.

♥ Make up signs on posterboards and leave them in conspicuous places (by stop signs or alongside the road) on a route your loved one travels regularly. (Just make sure that you have permission of the landowner or authorities to put them up and then be sure to remove them in a timely manner!)

♥ Write a sexy note and leave it in your love's favorite underwear.

♥ Create giant banners with your computer and printer that say things like "I Love You," "Welcome Home," and "I'm Upstairs Waiting for You," and put them all over the house. For an added festive touch, you might even gift-wrap yourself for when that certain party gets home!

♥ Find a local company that creates fake newspapers, and have them print one with a heading that says " 'I Love [His/Her Name] for ever and ever!' states [Your Name] Passionately." Leave it in a conspicuous place for your lover to find.

♥ Send ten, twenty, or more carefully chosen cards (one for each day, month, or year you have been together) saying "I love you and all the wonder and love you bring into my life." You can send them one at a time or (my personal favorite) all at once.

♥ When you are away on a business trip, send your loved one a postcard a day, written so that together they sequentially will spell out a special message when read. Follow them up with a reply card so he or she can respond.

♥ Create a scrapbook of your life together. It might have pictures and drawings,

include poetry and love letters, and/or be a story (perhaps including predictions of your joint future). No matter which format you choose, the result will be a memento you will both cherish.

♥ Have a mug, shirt, or keychain made with a picture of either the two of you, or just you, as a daily reminder of how special your relationship is.

♥ Dedicate a love song to your mate via his or her favorite radio station.

♥ Make a special cassette recording of your loved one's favorite songs/music and introduce them yourself, making the appropriate dedications. He or she will cherish that tape for years to come

♥ Frame the words to a mutually favorite song, and give it to your companion as a gift.

♥ Serenade your loved one with your "special" love song, or a song with his or her name in it, or even one you wrote just for him or her. The embarrassment will be well worth it.

♥ Create a personal calendar just for your significant other. Include pictures of yourself, perhaps in poses and attire he or she will particularly like, for each month— and highlight all the important dates.

♥ Send a poem that you wrote just for her or him. It doesn't even have to be good— just thoughtful and personal.

♥ Have special wineglasses made with your names or initials engraved on them. These most surely will let your mate know you care. (Don't forget to make up a special toast to dedicate to your love!)

♥ Give her a bottle of her favorite bubble bath. You might even surprise her by having a bubble bath ready, complete with a glass of champagne or a cup of hot tea, when she arrives home. Bath shops are chock full of other very personal gift ideas as well.

♥ Give her a bottle of her favorite perfume, or him a bottle of his favorite cologne or aftershave, along with a personalized love note.

♥ Present your loved one with a bottle of scented massage oil—and offer a massage with which to demonstrate it.

♥ Give your chosen one a copy of anything (book, audio cassette, or video cassette) by Leo Buscaglia.

♥ Surprise your loved one by buying his or her favorite "take-out" and bringing it home when he or she has had a particularly rough day. Remember to provide the appropriate beverage.

♥ Present your partner with an award (it doesn't have to be a trophy) inscribed with "World's Greatest Husband/Wife/Lover/[Whatever]."

♥ Honor him or her with a medal inscribed "For [Whatever] Above and Beyond the Call of Duty." A few suggestions are "Romantic Actions," "Loving," "Chivalry," "Gallantry," "Beauty," and "Loving Gentleness."

You show how much you care through both the gifts and services that you give and the way in which you give them; through the actions you take to bring your beloved happiness during the course of the day (and night); and by the way you let your loved one know how important he or she is to you and how lucky you feel to have him or her in your life!

Truly Romantic Gifts

nlike love, some things in life, though not free, are a whole lot of fun anyway—especially when enjoyed with your loved one.

Romantic gifts such as the following make for wonderful moments together (and even better memories), especially when they focus on something your lover desires. Romantic gift ideas you might consider sharing with him or her could include:

♥ Surprising your loved one by taking a course that will teach you to do something which excites that special person and that he or she can enjoy the rewards of with you—such as a cooking class, dancing lessons, instructions on giving sensual massages, or lessons on how to play a musical instrument. You can thus share your passion with your partner. Better yet, arrange for your partner to take a course that he or she would like.

♥ Surprising her by having her picked up (by cab or limousine) and taken for a day of absolute fantasy and pampering at a spa or an elegant beauty salon for a massage, full facial complete with makeup makeover, body wrap, manicure, pedicure, and hair styling.

♥ Surprising him by having him (and a friend—you?) picked up, taken to his favorite event (auto racing, a computer show, a football game), and shown to a great seating area.

♥ Having a surprise lunch delivered to her or his office. (Don't forget the love note!)

♥ Brown-bagging a lunch made up of some of her or his favorite foods (and including a love letter).

♥ Surprising her or him with a wonderful dinner you created yourself—complete with flowers, wine, carefully selected music, and the time to enjoy her or his company.

♥ Naming a star after your loved one (the International   Star Registry can help you out), complete with certificate and star map. Point out your personal star's star during an evening stroll!

♥ Planning a creative surprise party for your sweetheart. (Surprise parties *can* be exciting if they are innovative.) Have you ever thought of having a stretch limousine pick you both up for a quiet evening out, and then stop for friends along the way who are holding signs asking to join you? By the time you got to your destination, you might have brought the entire party with you!

♥ Planning a "scavenger hunt" of entertainment for your loved one. Select (and arrange for) special romantic settings that he or she would enjoy—like dinner on the beach, followed by front-row seats at a comedy show or play, then a stop at a favorite dessert spot, and finally home for an evening of fun. And ask the maître d' (or the equivalent) at each stop to tease her or him with riddles providing clues as to your next destination. It all can be wonderfully suspenseful and exciting! (Remember: It is the little details that make the hunt romantic.)

♥ Sending your kids either to camp or to a friend's house for the weekend, and pretending you are single and carefree again.

♥ Giving your loved one a bouquet made up of individually wrapped flowers that can be shared with others (people at the office, for instance) on a special occasion, such as Valentines Day. Not only will she or he be pleased and happy with the

knowledge that you thought of her or him, but also your gesture will give the added joy of allowing your love to make others happy.

♥ Sending a bouquet of specially selected helium-filled balloons, at least one of which has a note in, or attached to, it expressing your love.

♥ Buying a special gift that he or she would truly love, and having it delivered by the local pizzeria along with your favorite pizza. (You would be surprised what you can hide if you "core out" enough pizza boxes and stack them!) Pizza-box gift ideas abound in this section of this book.

♥ Giving her earrings and/or a necklace, worn by her favorite stuffed animal, or having your gift presented at a restaurant on a covered dish.

♥ Finding a gift that will make your loved one's collection of whatever more complete.

♥ Giving a gift that says more than just the gift itself—such as a music box that plays your song, or a bracelet with an inscription that might read "Our love is as perfect as this circle." You also could consider giving a wristwatch inscribed with "I think of you all the time," or a ring with your initials (perhaps separated by a heart) on it. Another suggestion might be a pen that reads "I love to hold you," or "You inspire me!"

♥ Surprising your loved one with a personalized license plate

♥ Commissioning a portrait of the two of you (or just of you) from your favorite photograph, and surprising your mate with it.

♥ Arranging to have a good supply of your loved one's favorite type of wine delivered. Purveyors of wine can help you to do this: Check your local telephone directory.

♥ Buying your lover a complete new outfit (down to underwear and shoes) and surprising him or her with it.

♥ Giving her or him a cassette player with auto-reverse and your favorite lovemaking music. (You don't want to have to stop in the middle of something special in order to turn the tape over, do you?)

♥ Enhancing your time together by giving him or her a hot tub. This could prove to be the most relaxing and sensual gift you'll ever give—in actuality, to both of you.

♥ Giving a gift that will become part of your daily lives such as "His and Her" robes, and beginning a new tradition: If either of you is "in the mood," the activist puts on his or her own robe. If both of you put on your robes, neither will remain that way for long.

Two words of caution apply as you finish this chapter: First, never give romantic gifts during a waning argument. Love tokens are _not_ a reward for not continuing to fight, but a way to say "I love you." Gifts should not be bribes. Second, always make sure you know what he or she likes and doesn't like as you plan your surprises.

As the old saying goes, "Plan to succeed, and you will." Planning doesn't take away from spontaneity. It actually enhances it by allowing you to flow with the moment rather than worry about details.

Timely Trivia

Have you ever wondered about what *else* happened during the year in which you were born (or your loved one was)? About the events that changed the course of history, the famous books that were published, the plays that were produced?

What may seem like birth-year trivia to others can be especially interesting to you when you receive a personalized birthday card citing highlights of "your" year. And the same goes for your loved one, no matter his or her age.

The following is a listing of outstanding events from 1920 through 1978. "Your" year, and/or that of your love, may well be shown here. (For more data about these and other years, see resource materials available in book stores, libraries, and stationery shops.)

1920   The League of Nations came into being.

        Edith Wharton wrote *The Age of Innocence*.

        American swimming champion Ethelda M. Bleibtrey was a three-time winner at the Antwerp Olympics.

        The American Professional Football Association was formed.

        Sugar Ray Robinson (who was to win five world boxing titles) was born.

1921   D. H. Lawrence wrote _Women in Love_.
Charlie Chaplin made _The Kid_.
Edvard Munch painted _The Kiss_.
The first radio account of a baseball game was broadcast from New York .
Radio station KDKA (Pittsburgh) began transmitting the first regular radio programs in the United States.

1922   James Joyce wrote _Ulysses_.
Mr. and Mrs. Dewitt Wallace founded _Reader's Digest_.
Irving Berlin wrote "April Showers."
Evans and Bishop discovered the antisterility Vitamin E.
Emily Post wrote _Etiquette_.

1923   Sigmund Freud wrote _The Ego and the Id_.
George Gershwin gave us "Rhapsody in Blue."
Mother's Day was first celebrated in Europe (after being recognized in the United States in 1907).
Paavo Nurmi ran the mile in four minutes.
Time magazine was founded by Henry Luce.

1924   The Pan-American Treaty was signed.
Robert Frost wrote "A Poem With Notes and Grace Notes."
E. M. Forster wrote A _Passage to India_.
Ford Motor Company produced their ten millionth car.
Rocky Marciano was born.
The first Winter Olympics was held in Chamonix, France.
J. Edgar Hoover became Director of the FBI.

1925   John Erskine wrote _The Private Life of Helen of Troy_.
John T. Scopes went on trial for teaching evolution.
The Chrysler Corporation was founded.
Madison Square Garden first opened in New York City.
Tennessee forbade sex education in its schools.

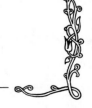

1926   Queen Elizabeth II was born.
The Book-of-the-Month Club was founded.
Duke Ellington's first records were pressed.
Robert Goddard fired the first liquid-fuel rocket.
Gertrude Ederle became the first woman to swim the English Channel.
Harry Houdini died as the result of a "trick" that went awry.
Most popular song: "I Found a Million-Dollar Baby in the Five-and-Ten Cent Store."

1927   Lev Theremin invented the earliest electronic musical instrument.
Charles Lindberg flew the single-engine monoplane *Spirit of St. Louis* from New York to Paris.
Josephine Baker became a star in Paris.
The Harlem Globetrotters basketball team was formed.
Johnny Weissmuller swam 100 yards in 51 seconds.

1928   D. H. Lawrence wrote *Lady Chatterley's Lover*.
Maurice Ravel composed *Bolero*.
Arturo Toscanini was named conductor of the New York Philharmonic Orchestra.
One of the more popular songs was "Makin' Whoopee."
Amelia Earhart became the first woman to fly (accompanied) across the Atlantic.
Shirley Temple was born.

1929   Ernest Hemingway wrote A *Farewell to Arms*.
Bertrand Russell wrote *Marriage and Morals*.
The first musical Mickey Mouse film was introduced.
The St. Valentine's Day Massacre took place.
The *Graf Zeppelin* flew around the world.

1930   Robert Frost wrote *Collected Poems*.
John Cowper Powys wrote his collection of essays entitled In *Defence of Sensuality*.

The movie *The Blue Angel*, starring Marlene Dietrich, was released.
Bobby Jones won the Grand Slam of golf.

1931   Disney released the first color movie, *Flowers and Trees*.
Clark Gable began his Hollywood career.
The Empire State Building was completed.
"The Star-Spangled Banner" became the United States' national anthem.
Al Capone was sent to jail for income-tax evasion.
Hattie T. Caraway became the first woman to be elected to the U.S. Senate.

1932   Franklin D. Roosevelt was elected President of the United States.
The Shakespeare Memorial Theatre opened in Stratford-Upon-Avon.
Amelia Earhart became the first woman to fly solo across the Atlantic.
Popular songs included "April in Paris" and "I'm Getting Sentimental Over You."

1933   Frances Perkins became the first woman member of the U.S. (presidential)
Cabinet.
Ulysses, by James Joyce, was finally allowed into the United States, after a court
ruling.
George Balanchine and Lincoln Kirstein founded the School of American Ballet.
Popular songs included "Smoke Gets in Your Eyes."
The first Baseball All-Star game was played.

1934   Best-sellers included *Goodbye Mr. Chips*.
Upton Sinclair wrote *The Book of Love*.
Sophia Loren was born.
The SS *Queen Mary* was launched.

1935   The U.S. Social Security Act was signed.
Jazz became known as "swing."
George Gershwin composed *Porgy and Bess*.
The longest bridge in the world, spanning the lower Zambesi, was opened to
traffic.
Elvis Presley was born.

1936   Dale Carnegie wrote *How to Win Friends and Influence People.*
Margaret Mitchell wrote *Gone With the Wind.*
Dr. Alexis Carrel developed the first artificial heart.
Jesse Owens won four Olympic Gold Medals in Berlin.
Henry Luce began publication of *Life* magazine.
The Baseball Hall of Fame was established.

1937   The U.S. Supreme Court ruled in favor of a minimum-wage law for women.
Compton MacKenzie wrote *The Four Winds of Love.*
The Golden Gate Bridge was opened for use.
The Duke of Windsor married Mrs. Wallis Simpson.
Joe Louis (Barrow) regained his heavyweight boxing title.

1938   Orson Welles's radio presentation "The War of the Worlds" (from the story by
      H. G. Wells) caused panic and flight in a number of areas.
Benny Goodman's band brought a new style to jazz.
The forty-hour work week was established in the United States.
Howard Hughes flew around the world.
The SS *Queen Elizabeth* was launched.
Don Budge won the Grand Slam of tennis.

1939   Pan-American began regular commercial service between Europe and the
      United States.
The first baseball game was televised in the United States.
Nylon stockings first appeared.
Gone With the Wind was made into a movie.

1940   Ernest Hemingway wrote *For Whom the Bell Tolls.*
Igor Stravinski composed his *Symphony in C.*
Winston Churchill gave his "blood, toil, tears, and sweat" speech (often quoted
      as "blood, sweat, and tears").
France's Lascaux caves were found to contain prehistoric wall paintings from
      approximately 20,000 B.C.
The first electron microscope was demonstrated.

1941   Winston Churchill wrote *Blood, Sweat and Tears*.

Manhattan Project research began.

Joe DiMaggio established a major-league record by hitting safely in 56 consecutive games.

The Monument Over Time Capsule, to be opened in 6939, was sealed and dedicated at the site of the 1939 New York World's Fair.

Construction of the Gatun Locks, Panama Canal, began.

The Rainbow Bridge over Niagara Falls was opened for use.

1942   Disney's *Bambi* and *Holiday Inn* (starring Bing Crosby) were two of the most popular films of the year.

Irving Berlin composed "White Christmas."

The first computer was developed in the United States.

The Mindenhall Treasure (a horde of Roman silverware) was discovered.

The first U.S. jet plane was tested.

1943   Rodgers and Hammerstein's *Oklahoma* won a special Pulitzer Prize.

The zoot suit (named thus in 1942) became popular in the United States.

William Howard Schuman composed *Secular Cantata No. 2, A Free Song*, and won the first Pulitzer Prize in music.

Casablanca won an Academy Award for Best Picture, and one for Best Director.

1944   Franklin D. Roosevelt was elected to his fourth consecutive term.

The first nonstop flight from London to Canada took place.

Aaron Copland composed *Appalachian Spring*, which won a Pulitzer Prize in music in 1945.

Leonard Bernstein's musical comedy *On the Town* opened in New York.

1945   Mary Chase wrote the Pulitzer Prize-winning *Harvey*.

Henry Green wrote *Loving*.

Nancy Milford wrote *The Pursuit of Love*.

World War II ended.

Fleming, Florey, and Chain shared the Nobel Prize in medicine, for the discovery of penicillin.

1946   Benjamin Spock, M.D., wrote *Baby and Child Care*.
        Joe Louis (Barrow) successfully defended his heavyweight title for the twenty-
            third time.
        Irving Berlin's musical comedy *Annie Get Your Gun* opened in New York.

1947   Tennessee Williams wrote A *Streetcar Named Desire*, which won a Pulitzer Prize in
            drama in 1948.
        Mickey Spillane's I, *the Jury* was published.
        The Dead Sea Scrolls from 22 B.C. to 100 A.D. were discovered.
        A U.S. airplane flew at supersonic speeds for the first time.
        The transistor was invented by Bell Laboratories.

1948   The 200-inch Mount Palomar reflecting telescope was dedicated.
        Idlewild Airport (renamed Kennedy Airport in 1963) was dedicated.
        Evelyn Waugh wrote *The Loved One*.
        Alfred C. Kinsey wrote *Sexual Behavior in the Human Male*.
        Joe Louis (Barrow) retired from boxing.

1949   Norman Vincent Peale wrote A *Guide to Confident Living*.
        Fulton Oursler wrote *The Greatest Story Ever Told*.
        Erich Fromm wrote *Man for Himself*.
        Rodgers and Hammerstein's musical play *South Pacific* opened in New York.
        One of the more popular songs was "Diamonds Are a Girl's Best friend."

1950   Tennessee Williams wrote *The Roman Spring of Mrs. Stone*.
        The world population grew to approximately 2.3 billion.
        The United Nations building in New York was completed.
        "Mona Lisa" was one of the most popular songs.
        All About Eve won three Academy Awards (Picture, Director, and Supporting
            Actor).
        Henri Matisse began work on the Vence Chapel.

1951   The bestselling book was *Desiree*, by Annemarie Selinko.
        Matisse completed work on the Vence Chapel.

An *American in Paris* won the Academy Award for Best Picture.
Frank Lloyd Wright designed the Friedman House in Pleasantville, New York.
Rodgers and Hammerstein's *The King and I* opened in New York.
One of the most popular songs was "Kisses Sweeter Than Wine."
The first consumer color TV was introduced in the United States.

1952   John Steinbeck wrote *East of Eden*.
Norman Vincent Peale wrote *The Power of Positive Thinking*.
The first effective contraceptive pill was produced.
Albert Schweitzer won the Nobel Peace Prize.
Rocky Marciano won the world heavyweight boxing title from "Jersey Joe" Walcott.
Christian Dior gained influence in the Parisian world of haute couture.
The U.S. won forty-three gold medals in the Helsinki Olympics.

1953   Ian Fleming wrote *Casino Royale*.
Winston Churchill won the Nobel Prize in literature.
George Axelrod wrote *The Seven-Year Itch*.
Simone de Beauvoir wrote *The Second Sex*.
Hillary and Tenzing become the first to climb Mount Everest.
Alfred C. Kinsey wrote *Sexual Behavior in the Human Female*.

1954   Ernest Hemingway won the Nobel Prize in literature.
Tennessee Williams wrote *Cat on a Hot Tin Roof*, which won a Pulitzer Prize for drama in 1955.
Thornton Wilder wrote *The Matchmaker*.
Dr. Jonas Salk began innoculating schoolchildren with his antipolio vaccine.
Roger Bannister ran a mile in 3 minutes 59.4 seconds.
Gordon Richards became the first professional jockey to be knighted.

1955   Vladimir Nabokov wrote *Lolita*.
Salvador Dalí completed *Sacrament of the Last Supper*.
One of the most popular songs was "Love Is a Many-Splendored Thing."
Commercial TV began broadcasting in Great Britain.

1956   Grace Metalious wrote *Peyton Place*.

John F. Kennedy wrote *Profiles in Courage*.

Alan Jay Lerner and Frederick Loewe's musical *My Fair Lady* opened in New York.

Elvis Presley became a household name.

An oral vaccine against polio was developed by Albert Sabin.

Bell Laboratories began to develop a "visual" telephone.

Prince Rainier of Monaco married Grace Kelly of Philadelphia.

"Rock and Roll" came into vogue.

The New York Coliseum opened.

Rocky Marciano retired, undefeated in fifty bouts, from boxing.

1957   Albert Camus won the Nobel Prize in literature.

Dr. Seuss wrote *The Cat in the Hat*.

Kenneth Clark completed *The Nude (A Study of Ideal Art)*.

Leonard Bernstein's musical *West Side Story* opened in New York.

The International Geophysical Year was proclaimed.

The number of cities with one million-plus populations grew to seventy-one (up from sixteen in 1914).

The Wolfenden Report (on homosexuality and prostitution) was published in Great Britain.

Thirteen-year-old Bobby Fischer emerged as a promising chess champion.

1958   The European Common Market came into being.

Truman Capote wrote *Breakfast at Tiffany's*.

Boris Pasternak wrote *Dr. Zhivago*.

Henry Moore completed his *Reclining Figure* at the UNESCO Building in Paris.

Cat on a Hot Tin Roof and *Gigi* were the top films of the year.

Samuel Barber won a Pulitzer Prize for his opera *Vanessa*.

NASA was established, and the United States launched its first "Moon rocket" (which didn't reach the Moon, but did travel 79,000 miles).

The Beatnik movement spread across the western world.

1959   Hawaii became the fiftieth state of the United States.

The New York City Council appointed a committee to study the idea of the City's becoming the fifty-first state.

Graham Greene wrote *The Complaisant Lover.*

Allen Drury wrote *Advise and Consent,* which won a Pulitzer Prize in 1960.

James Michener wrote *Hawaii.*

Ian Fleming wrote *Goldfinger.*

"The Sound of Music" was one of the most popular songs.

The first synthetic diamond was created by DeBeers.

U.S. Postmaster General Summerfield banned D. H. Lawrence's *Lady Chatterly's Lover* on grounds of obscenity (the ruling was reversed in 1960 by court order).

Jack Nicklaus won the U.S. Golf Association's Amateur-class championship.

1960   John F. Kennedy was elected President of the United States.

Errol Flynn's *My Wicked, Wicked Ways* was published posthumously.

Harper Lee wrote *To Kill a Mockingbird,* which won a Pulitzer Prize in 1961.

C. P. Snow wrote *The Affair.*

Gore Vidal wrote *The Best Man.*

Psycho, The Apartment, and *Exodus* were among the most popular movies of the year.

Churchill College in Cambridge was founded.

1961   John F. Kennedy was inaugurated as the youngest President in U.S. history.

The Peace Corps was established.

Henry Miller's *The Tropic of Cancer* finally was published in the United States.

Harold Robbins wrote *The Carpetbaggers.*

One of the most popular songs was "Love Makes the World Go 'Round."

The Orient Express made its last journey from Paris to Bucharest.

Alan B. Shepard Jr. made the first manned U.S. space flight.

1962   John Steinbeck won the Nobel Prize in literature.

Aleksandr Solzhenitsyn's *One Day in the Life of Ivan Denisovich* was published.

Edward Albee wrote _Who's Afraid of Virginia Woolf?_
Ken Kesey wrote _One Flew Over the Cuckoo's Nest._
Astronauts Glenn, Carpenter, and Schirra orbited Earth.

1963   Winston Churchill became an honorary citizen of the United States.
Leonardo da Vinci's _Mona Lisa_ was exhibited in New York and in Washington, D.C.
The Berlin Philharmonic was organized by Hans Scharoun.
Joan Baez and Bob Dylan were the most popular singers of the year.
Valentina Tereshkova became the first female astronaut in space.
Dr. Michael De Bakey used the first artificial heart in a surgical operation, allowing it to pump blood for the body while the real heart was being operated on.

1964   Martin Luther King was awarded the Nobel Peace Prize.
Cezanne's _Les Grandes Baigneuses_ was acquired by the National Gallery in London.
The Gallery of Modern Art opened in New York.
Elizabeth Taylor married Richard Burton for the first time.
My Fair Lady won Academy Awards for Best Picture, Director, and Best Actor.
Jerry Herman's musical comedy _Hello, Dolly_ opened in New York.
Cassius Clay (later Muhammad Ali) won the heavyweight boxing title from Sonny Liston.
The Watusi, Monkey, Funky Chicken, and Twist dances were in vogue.

1965   Picasso completed his _Self-Portrait._
The Sound of Music won Academy Awards for Best Picture and Director.
Charles Chaplin and Ingmar Bergman were awarded the Dutch Erasmus Prize.
U.S. Astronaut Edward White and Russian Cosmonaut Aleksei Leonov walked in space on separate missions (the Russian first).
World production of diamonds totaled 342,000 karats.

1966   Jacques Brel wrote _L'Adoration._
Jacqueline Susann wrote _Valley of the Dolls._

Van Gogh's portrait of Mlle Ravoux sold for $441,000.

The first U.S. spacecraft (Surveyor) landed on the Moon.

The Salazar Suspension Bridge (fifth-longest in the world) opened for use in Lisbon.

Miniskirts came into fashion.

Color TV became very popular.

The U.S. population grew to 195,827,000.

Jim Ryun ran the mile in 3 minutes 51.3 seconds.

1967   Ira Levin wrote *Rosemary's Baby*.

Charles de Quintrec's book of French poetry, *Stances de verbs amour*, was published.

Robert K. Massie wrote *Nicholas and Alexandra*.

Leonardo da Vinci's portrait of Ginevra de Benci was acquired by the National Gallery in Washington for $6 million.

Barbra Streisand sang for 135,000 fans in Central Park, New York.

Singer Gerry Dorsey changed his name to Engelbert Humperdinck and gained world fame.

Dr. Christiaan Barnard performed the world's first human heart transplant.

Peggy Fleming won the World Championship in women's figure skating in Vienna.

David Frost emerged as "Television Personality of the Year."

Twiggy took the U.S. fashion industry by storm.

1968   John Updike wrote *Couples*.

Arthur Hailey wrote *Airport*.

Neil Simon wrote his famous play *Plaza Suite*.

Muriel Spark wrote *The Prime of Miss Jean Brodie*.

Norton Simon paid $1.55 million for *Le Pont des Arts* by Renoir.

Mickey Mouse celebrated his fortieth birthday.

World production of wine during the year was 269.3 million hectoliters.

Jacqueline Kennedy married Aristotle Onassis.

The "midi" failed to replace the "mini" in fashion circles.

Peggy Fleming won the only U.S. Gold Medal at the Winter Olympics.

1969   Philip Roth wrote *Portnoy's Complaint*.

Mario Puzo wrote *The Godfather*.

Lillian Hellman wrote *An Unfinished Woman*.

Harold Robbins received a $2.5 million advance for his novel *The Inheritor*.

Jacqueline Susann wrote *The Love Machine*.

The New York sex revue *Oh! Calcutta!* opened.

The three-hundredth anniversary of the death of Rembrandt was noted widely.

Pants outfits became acceptable for everyday wear by women.

The Concorde made its first real test flight.

Neil Armstrong became the first man to walk on the Moon.

Rod Laver won the Grand Slam of tennis for the second time.

1970   Soviet novelist Aleksandr Solzhenitsyn won the Nobel Prize in literature.

Neil Simon wrote *Last of the Red Hot Lovers*.

Jim Bouton wrote *Ball Four*.

Elliott Gould emerged as the year's most successful film star.

Burt Bacharach became famous with the help of his two Academy Awards, one for his musical score for *Butch Cassidy and the Sundance Kid*, and the other for his song "Raindrops Keep Falling on My Head."

The 150-inch telescopes at Kitt Peak Observatory (Tucson, Arizona) and the Inter-American Observatory (Chile) were completed.

1971   Erich Segal wrote *Love Story*.

John Updike wrote *Rabbit Redux*.

Conceptual art became a major craze in America.

The Metropolitan Museum paid $5,544,000 for a portrait by Velázquez.

Cigarette ads were banned from U.S. television.

Rolls-Royce, Ltd., declared bankruptcy.

Henry "Hank" Aaron hit his six-hundredth career home run.

Legalized offtrack betting was introduced in New York.

Amtrak began passenger operations.

1972   *Fiddler on the Roof*, the longest-running show in Broadway history to that point
      in time, closed after 3,242 performances.
    Tom O'Horgan directed *Jesus Christ, Superstar*.
    Norton Simon paid $3 million for *Madonna and Child* by Raphael.
    Leonard Bernstein conducted *Mass* in Washington, D.C.
    The Soviet spacecraft Venus 8 landed on Venus.
    American swimmer Mark Spitz captured a record seven Olympic Gold Medals.
    Clifford Irving concocted his Howard Hughes "biography."
    The Star of Sierra Leone, a diamond weighing 969.8 karats, the largest ever
      found, was unearthed.
    Bobby Fischer won the world chess title.
    The Dow-Jones Index closed above the 1,000 mark for the first time in history.

1973   A New York Criminal Court judge ruled that *Deep Throat* was "indisputably and
      irredeemably obscene."
    Last Tango in Paris, starring Marlon Brando, was one of the hottest movies of
      the year.
    Secretariat won horse-racing's Triple Crown.
    Billie Jean King defeated Bobby Riggs in tennis's "Battle of the Sexes."
    The Godfather won Academy Awards for Best Picture and Best Actor.

1974   Aleksandr Solzhenitsyn was stripped of his Soviet citizenship and sent into
      exile.
    Solzhenitsyn finished writing *The Gulag Archipelago: 1918—1956* despite
      setbacks.
    John Le Carre wrote *Tinker, Tailor, Soldier, Spy*.
    Muhammad Ali reclaimed the heavyweight boxing championship for the
      second of his three times.
    Henry "Hank" Aaron passed Babe Ruth's record of 714 home runs.
    "Streaking" became a fad in the United States.
    Little League Baseball voted to allow girls to play on its teams.
    Frank Robinson became the manager of the Cleveland Indians major league
      baseball team.

1975   Six thousand life-sized pottery figures from the third century B.C. were
            discovered in northern China.
        A _Chorus Line_ was named Best Musical by New York drama critics.
        Beverly Sills sang Rossini's _The Siege of Corinth_ in her Metropolitan Opera debut.
        The United States' _Viking_ unmanned spacecraft was sent on a 500-million-mile
            trip to Mars to seek signs of life.
        The American _Apollo_ and Soviet _Soyuz_ spacecraft linked up, 140 miles above
        Earth, and their crews shared a handshake and a meal.
        Charles Chaplin was knighted by Queen Elizabeth II.
        Mrs. Junko Tabei, a thirty-five-year-old Japanese woman, became the first
            woman to successfully climb Mt. Everest.
        John Walker ran the mile in 3 minutes, 49.4 seconds.
        First Women's Bank opened in New York City.

1976   A _Chorus Line_ won both a Pulitzer Prize and a Tony Award.
        Alex Haley wrote _Roots_.
        Carl Bernstein and Bob Woodward wrote _The Final Days_.
        One Flew Over the Cuckoo's Nest won all five major Academy Awards—the first film
            to do so since 1934.
        Rocky was one of the most popular films of the year.
        Henry "Hank" Aaron retired as a professional baseball player with a record of
            755 career home runs (Babe Ruth had 714 on retirement).

1977   Colleen McCullough wrote _The Thorn Birds_.
        Martin Charnin's _Annie_ won the New York Drama Critics and Tony Awards for
            best musical.
        Elvis Presley, "The King of Rock and Roll," died.
        Amnesty International won the Nobel Peace Prize.
        Rocky won Academy Awards for Best Picture and Director.
        Star Wars was one of the most popular movies of the year.
        The 2,300-year-old tomb of King Philip II of Macedon, father of Alexander the
            Great, was found in northern Greece.
        A miniplanet was discovered circling the sun between Saturn and Uranus.

For the first time in history, a life-threatening viral infection (herpes encephalitis) was successfully treated with drugs.

Cindy Nicholas became the first woman to complete a round-trip swim across the English Channel.

The Concorde began passenger service among New York, Paris, and London.

The official U.S. population reached the 216 million mark.

1978   A Gutenberg Bible sold for $2 million.

James Michener wrote *Chesapeake.*

Annie Hall won the Academy Award for best picture.

The first "test-tube baby" was born in England.

A moon was discovered orbiting Pluto.

Muhammad Ali beat Leon Spinks to regain the heavyweight boxing title for the third (and final) time in his boxing career.

King Hussein married Elizabeth Halaby.

The world's population reached 4.4 billion people.

When Love Story, a film based on the 1970 novel of the same name by Erich Segal, was shown on TV, it was watched by 72 million people, the largest audience (to that time) for one televised movie.

The Gift of Time

There is no greater gift that we can give our loved one than the gift of time, especially when it is spent personalizing a gift, a thought, or an action.

This is especially true when you celebrate his/her birthday, that annual reminder of the joy of having someone in our life who loves us. And what better way is there to celebrate such an auspicious event than to give our dearest companion the benefit of our wisdom?

The following quotes (made about those special ages we all hold dear) are respectfully submitted for your perusal and for possible use (and modification) in your loved one's birthday cards. Enjoy!

Eighteen is a wondrous year,
full of hope yet free of fear.

Nineteen is a time of thought,
dreaming of treasures to be sought.

Twenty offers peace of mind,
the teenage years are left behind.

Twenty-one comes only once,
a time for youthful "exuberance."

Twenty-two is an interesting age,
the introduction to life's living stage.

Twenty-three is an open door,
hinting of the future that life holds in store.

Twenty-four is a time of change,
some of which feels heavenly and some very strange.

Twenty-five is a special treat,
the first life-transition now complete.

Twenty-six brings inner reflection,
emphasizing the need to have a set direction.

Twenty-seven is glory-bound,
promising untold treasures to be found.

Twenty-eight holds a marvelous attraction,
for those who enjoy a life of action.

Twenty-nine is an affectionate year,
loved by many who thirty fear.

Thirty is the time in life,
when self-assurance ends emotional strife.

Thirty-five brings confusion to an end,
maturity now a newfound friend.

Forty sees wisdom near,
though foolhardiness is still held dear.

Forty-five fosters joy complete,
a member now of an age elite.

Fifty judges our life's refrain,
whether lived with joy or filled with pain.

Fifty-five starts life anew,
a special reward for those who grew.

Sixty is the age to be,
financially, mentally, and emotionally free.

Sixty-five is a special rite,
bringing peace and pure delight.

Seventy's praises should be sung,
knowing living has just begun.

The years that follow are full of grace,
treasured moments defining our place.

—Michael Newman

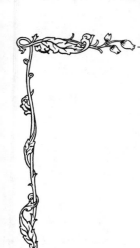

Playful Aphrodisiacs

he quest for aphrodisiacs (named after Aphrodite, Greek goddess of love and beauty) is as old as humankind, even though most substances referred to as such seldom have delivered as promised or expected. Usually the results have been more psychological. In fact, one of the first celebrated aphrodisiacs was salt because it was associated with Aphrodite, who was said to have come from the sea (a belief which continued well into the Middle Ages). Here are some other historical facts on this subject:

♥ Most of the earliest aphrodisiacs were foods that resembled human sexual organs. The belief was that eating these would increase one's ability to perform sexually. This class of foods included asparagus, bananas, beets, carrots, clams, cucumbers, eggs, figs, oysters, turnips, and even the powdered horn of a rhinoceros. One such belief centered around Aristotle and his contemporaries, who were convinced that eating beans (any beans) created lust in human beings.

♥ A variation on this theme, played out in ancient Syracuse, involved the downing of cakes made in the shape of female sexual organs. This practice became common in medieval times as well®especially in Germany and England. Indeed, the quest for the ultimate aphrodisiac was to prove never-ending.

♥ Ecclesiastes refers to the caper berry as causing lust in its user. Mandrake as an aphrodisiac is also mentioned in the Old Testament (in Genesis and in the Song of Solomon), as is (in Exodus) the root of sweet flag when chewed or made into a tea.

♥ Ancient Greeks and Romans believed that apples symbolized eros, and gave them as gifts to their loved ones. Ancient Scandinavians believed that their gods experienced both rejuvenation and increased sexual potency by eating apples, and therefore considered their consumption to be the key to increasing amorous activity.

♥ Alchemists in the Middle Ages sold aphrodisiacs that included powdered gold or pearls as a key ingredient. Another medieval aphrodisiac recipe involved dried black ants soaked in oil.

♥ Eighteenth-century France considered parmesan cheese to be an extremely effective aphrodisiac. France was also reknowned for its "green muse" made from the herb wormwood. It was considered to be a very powerful aphrodisiac. Even today, wormwood is thought to have lust-enhancing qualities.

♥ Albertus Magnus, a renowned theologian and scientist as well as teacher of Thomas Aquinas, believed that powdered partridge brains steeped in red wine was the ultimate aphrodisiac.

Today, there is a wide variety of herbs, plants, and other foods that are thought to act as aphrodisiacs. There is also an expanded appreciation for the aphrodisiacal qualities of nurturing your lover's other senses.

The Roman poet Ovid summed it up best when, in offering advice on love to his fellow countrymen, he concluded that the best way for a man to attract a woman was to take regular baths, have a nice suntan, brush his teeth, dress nicely, and be neatly groomed. The best means available to a woman to attract a gentleman was to arrange her hair in a pleasing manner, move gracefully, be demure, and dress in such a way as to emphasize the most pleasing aspects of her shape and coloring.

Some of the more efficacious ways of increasing sexual desire in your loved one are to share aromatic baths, give each other massages, read books of love together, and go dancing. (In fact, dancing can be the ultimate aphrodisiac when done erotical-

Eighteenth-century English brothels served meals to their clients that were made up of foods and drinks thought to have a positive effect on amorous desire and increase sexual performance.

ly.) Gifts known to stimulate amorous behavior also include flowers and precious stones. The right music, a touch of an especially appealing perfume or cologne worn in just the right spot, and the wearing of clothing your loved one finds sensual, act as aphrodisiacs, too. Of course, hugging and kissing your loved one will almost invariably lead to some sort of amorous activity.

Foods and other culinary ingredients that are considered to have aphrodisiacal effects include almonds, anise, anvalli nuts, artichokes, asparagus, bamboo shoots, basil, black pepper, black walnuts, wild cabbage, caraway, cardamom, caviar, celery, cherries, chestnuts, chutney, cinnamon, cumin, curry, dill, endives, eryngo, fennel, fish (any kind), garlic, ginger, honey, horseradish, juniper berries, marjoram, mint, mugwort, mustard seeds, nutmeg, onion seeds, paprika, pimentos, pine seeds, pistachio nuts, rosemary, saffron, sage, seafood (all kinds), tarragon, thyme, truffles, and vanilla. The best-known of these, the extract of the root of a high-quality ginseng plant, is known to restore sexual vitality when chewed, made into a tea, or taken in pill form. Share some with your loved one!

Other, less accessible herbs, plants, and trees that are also reputed to be aphro-disiacs include the nuts of the betel tree, tea made from the leaves of the damiana shrub, tea made from the herb fo-ti-tieng (known as the "elixir of long life" in the Far East), coffee made from the seeds of the guarana shrub, tea made from the bark of the muira-puama tree, tea made from the bark of the American black willow, and tea made from certain parts of the yohimbe tree.

For the ultimate romantic evening, plan an after-hours menu with a few of these special foods. Even though their aphrodisiacal powers may be questionable, you can

both still enjoy their "magical" powers.

While any or all of the preceding aids to amour may help intensify your love life together, the most powerful aphrodisiac of all is still (and will always be) the mind. It is your *mind* that generates the love you feel toward another, and the desire that you experience when you are with the one you love. But always be aware that it is romance that ties it all together. In the immortal words of the Roman poet Ovid, "To be loved, be lovable." And romance is the key to *staying* in love!

Erotica

he word *erotica* comes from the name of the Greek god Eros, the God of Erotic Love (who was known to the Romans as Cupid). It refers to ideas, activities, situations, and the like that stimulate us sexually as well as romantically by tantalizing all our senses.

While most of the chapters in this book are filled with erotic suggestions on how to make you and your loved one's love life better, certain ideas truly deserve a special forum all their own. Some of these include:

Passionate Games

Games are a wonderful way to nurture intimacy between two lovers, especially when they allow touching, sharing, and open communication. The six most popular romantic games for two people in love are:

♥ "An Enchanting Evening" by Games Partnership, Ltd.

♥ "The Game—Charades—Fun Through the Art of Communication" by John M. Hansen Company

♥ "Love Dice" by Schocal

♥ "Love Potion No. 9—A Sensual Massage Game for Two" by The Game Works

♥ "Lovers and Liars" by Ty Wilson, Ltd.

♥ "Recipe for Romance" by The Game Works

   Other popular adult games that can be played with others include:

♥ "Dirty Minds" by TDC Games

♥ "Dirty Money—The Game of Indecent Proposals" by TDC Games

♥ "Dirty Words—The Card Game" by Matscot International, Inc.

♥ "Sexual Secrets—The Game of Intimate Confessions" by TDC Games

♥ "Sexual Trivia—The Tuxedo Edition" by Matscot International, Inc.

♥ "Talk Dirty to Me" by TDC Games

♥ "X-Rated Charades" by The Game Works

   All of these can be found at most stores that specialize in games.

Dressed for Success

If you prefer a game with no rules that is a little more personal in nature, you might consider playing "dress-up." It's one of the most predictable/unpredictable games you'll ever play. Sound confusing? Well, it shouldn't. Look at it this way: Although the final outcome of the game is virtually assured, chances are you'll be surprised at how many different ways you can arrive at it—and *that* is what makes "dress-up" so much fun. All it takes is the right kind of clothes.

   One great place for a woman to start would be a local women's apparel store that specializes in (or has a department that specializes in) women's undergarments. Very little turns most men on more than having the woman they love greet them at the door attired only in lingerie! A great place for a man would be the local tuxedo shop or costume shop. There is (especially to the woman who loves him) something truly sensual about a man dressed in a tuxedo or uniform, as a construction worker, or in sexy pajamas. Talk to your loved one and find out what kind of "dress-up" fantasy would turn her or him on, and then change it to reality.

If you are uncomfortable about visiting your local lingerie shop, there are two companies that have catalog departments in addition to their store service: Victoria's Secret (800-888-8200) and Fredrick's of Hollywood (800-323-9525). Victoria's Secret specializes in a very feminine approach to women's lingerie that is alluring in its sensuality, yet (because it leaves something to the imagination) is deadly in its aim. For couples who prefer to wear something a little more erotic, Frederick's of Hollywood offers an assortment of sexy women's *and* men's clothing designed to excite you by allowing you a peek at the pleasures that await you.

If you would like an even greater variety of choices, you can call Intimate Treasures, a San Francisco-based company that specializes in catalogs and videos, at 415-896-0944. They can arrange to get you catalogs from companies that sell sexy lingerie of all types, including Bedroom Fantasies, Chippendales, Lovelace, Playboy, and Sophisticated Intimates (to name only a few).

Erotic Delicacies

The perfect way to finish a game of "dress-up" would be to smother your loved one's body with kisses as you undressed her or him, or even cover her/his body with chocolate (or some other wonderful dessert) and lick it off—assuming of course that your paramour wasn't wearing edible underwear, which offers even more interesting possibilities.

Of course, there are other forms of chocolate "desserts." After all, that wonderful stuff is known to have aphrodisiac powers! Fortunately, nearly every city has shops that specialize in chocolate roses and hand-made truffles, all which are designed to open your lover's heart to your passionate advances. They may also offer erotically shaped chocolate candies for couples who prefer something a little more suggestive, if not more artistic.

If you are looking for something sweet and sexy but a little different, you might try a bakery that specializes in erotic cookies, pastries, and cakes. Tell them what you have in mind, and chances are they can help you out—whether it be long-stemmed chocolate chip roses or a suggestive cake awaiting your loved one as he or she comes home and realizes, to his/her delight, that *you* are the main course, and the cake is both dessert and the map to your mutual pleasure!

"Wow, Do You Look Fantastic!"

If you would like to try something really different, have a photographer take a picture of you in a highly provocative pose and give it to your loved one as a gift. He or she will get sexually excited every time he/she looks at it. If you prefer something a little less obvious, you might have a glamour shot taken. Either way, special thoughts of you will fill your sweetie's mind every time your image is the object of his or her attention.

Finally, no chapter on erotica would be complete without a mention of Madonna, the Queen of eroticism—thanks largely to her book of personal erotic photographs, *Sex*, and to her 1992 album, *Erotica*. Talk about aphrodisiacs!

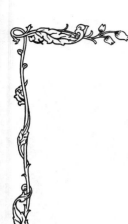

Tantalizing Aromas

Hippocrates, the Greek physician known as "the father of modern medicine," said, "The way to health is to have an aromatic bath and scented massage every day." He knew that good overall health involved having a healthy body *and* a sound mind. He was aware (as were the ancient Egyptians from as far back as 4500 B.C.) that essential oils affect and benefit the mind as well as the body when used in massage oils and in baths, and even when inhaled. In fact, this knowledge was so common that aromatherapy (ie., the beneficial use of essential oils) also was routinely practiced by the Arabic, Chinese, Greek, Hebrew, and Indian civilizations of long ago much as it is today.

Essential oils are the aromatic substances found in most wild and cultivated plants alike. While most plants provide only one essential oil, and that usually in minute quantities, some plants (and trees) offer much more—such as the orange tree, which provides orange (in the skin of the fruit), petitgrain (in the leaves), and neroli (in the orange blossoms)—each very different from the other, both in smell and in therapeutic properties.

The one thing all essential oils have in common is a group of antibiotic, antiseptic, anti-inflammatory, and antiviral properties that can variously enhance your mood, depending on which one(s) you use. This is to say that essential oils can be used in a variety of ways. Lovers usually

choose to use them either in massage oils (the most effective way), add them to warm baths that they share, or inhale them (either as incense, from a candle, or as part of a vapor mist) as they make love.

Translations of the hieroglyphics found on papyri in the Temple of Edfu, on the Papyrus of Ebers, and on the Papyrus of Edwin Smith indicate that the high priests of their time period used aromatic substances to make both perfumes and medicinal potions, and that aromatherapy was an important part of both their pharmacology and their pathology. The papyri contained a number of aromatic mixtures that were designed to treat certain illnesses, such as hay fever, and prevent conception and restore youth.

The most common essential oils used by lovers include:

♥ *Benzoin*—which by scent is reminiscent of vanilla and is often used in perfumes. It is usually combined with almond oil when used as a massage oil, and is supposed to drive away loneliness and anxiety when used this way. Whether used in incense or in massage oil, it is supposed to both relax and invigorate you.

♥ *Bergamot*—which belongs to the orange tree family. It has a lovely emerald color and a lemon scent. Whether used as incense, in a bath, or as a massage oil, it uplifts your and your loved one's spirits by driving away anxiety and depression. It is considered to be the aromatherapist's most valuable oil.

♥ *Cardamom*—which comes from the distillation of seeds found in the fruits of various plants belonging to the ginger family. It is either colorless or slightly yellow in color, and has a sweet, warm aroma. It is used widely in India as an aphrodisiac when taken orally, or in a bath, for lovers.

♥ *Chamomile*—which was considered to be a sacred flower in ancient Egypt and was offered to Ra, the Egyptian Sun God, to please him. It has a beautiful blue color when first distilled that eventually becomes greenish-yellow and has an apple-like scent. Usually combined with rosemary and soya oil in massage oils, it has a calming affect as it relieves muscle pains when rubbed in. It is an effective stimulant when added to bath water and a relaxing, refreshing drink when used to make tea. No matter which form you and your loved one use Camomile oil in, it will relieve both your stress and your stress- related symptoms. Since it is one of the gentler essential oils, it can be used by everyone.

♥ *Cedarwood*—which is a yellowish essential oil that has a warm, woody fragrance. It can be inhaled, used in your bath, or referred to as a massage oil; and it is known for both its wonderful effect on skin and for its aphrodisiac properties.

♥ *Clary Sage*—which has a wonderful nutty aroma and tastes like muscatel wine. When used in a massage oil, it is extremely relaxing and does a great job of relieving stress and tension. It also leaves your loved one with a feeling of euphoria and is thought to have aphodisiacal properties.

♥ *Frankincense*—which is a yellowish essential oil with a balsamic aroma. Used as incense in religious ceremonies for centuries it is known for its calming effect on the body. When it is used in a bath, it is known to relieve stress and will leave both you and your loved one relaxed.

♥ *Geranium*—which has a strong but agreeable aroma similar to that of rose but can best be described as "green," much like its color. It has very powerful antidepressant properties and is thought to help with the healing process when used in massage oils.

♥ *Jasmine*—which is considered to be the king of essential oils. Dark in color, it has a very heavy aroma. Jasmine has had a reputation as an aphrodisiac since the days of antiquity, probably because it is so effective in relieving tension and anxiety while it warms your loved one as he or she is being massaged with this wonderful oil. It is also fantastic for skin care.

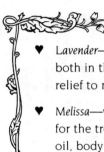

♥ *Lavender*—which is one of the most versatile of all essential oils. It is very effective both in the treatment of skin problems, including acne and burns, and for bringing relief to muscles—especially when used as a massage oil or in a bath.

♥ *Melissa*—which is basically a colorless essential oil with a lemony aroma. Wonderful for the treatment of anxiety and depression, it can be taken orally or used as a bath oil, body oil, or massage oil.

♥ *Neroli*—which is obtained by distilling the fresh flowers of an orange tree. It has a yellowish color and has a wondrous effect on the the central nervous system, effectively treating anxiety and depression. Taken orally, it acts as a natural traquilizer. It will also relax your whole body when it is used in your bath or in massage oil. It is believed to act as an aphrodisiac.

♥ *Orange*—which comes from the skin of an orange and has an orange coloring. Like its cousin neroli, it is a wonderful antidepressant and can be used as a mild sedative, yet it is a "warmer" oil and seems to be preferred in colder weather.

♥ *Petitgrain*—which has a soft, flowery scent and is a wonderfully refreshing bath oil as well as a very good massage oil. It is effective in reducing mild cases of stress (neroli is much better for cases of anxiety) and leaves a very soothing and delicate aroma.

♥ *Rose*—which has been the perfume of royalty and pharaohs throughout history. It is referred to as the queen of all essential oils. Besides being good for skin problems, it is considered to be an effective sexual stimulant for women, especially when used in a body oil or massage oil.

♥ *Sandalwood*—which is best known for its use as a perfume, and almost as importantly for its aphrodisiacal qualities. It is also effective in skin care when used in a massage oil.

♥ *Ylang Ylang*—which is a yellowish essential oil that has an exquisite aroma. Its reputation is based on its purported ability to ease anxiety and to act as an aphrodisiac. It can be added to bath water and used in massage oils or as a perfume.

All of these essential oils, as well as others, are most effective when they are biologically natural (as opposed to the synthetic variations that can be found on the market).

The best way to savor the benefits of aromatherapy is to check out the array of massage oils, scented candles, incense sticks, vapor oils, bath oils, and body oils available at most shops that specialize in aromatic supplies. Experimenting with various aromas and qualities of oil will help you and your loved one find the one that brings the most pleasure to your lovemaking. And using these mood enhancers will bring your relationship to a level of intimacy you never dreamed possible.

You will find that, by heightening the awareness of the fifth of your five senses during your lovemaking, your love life will explode in sheer ecstasy!

Sensual Seduction

Sensual seduction is much, much more than foreplay. It is the giving of absolute pleasure to your loved one, as you slowly and tenderly eliminate all stress from his or her body and mind, filling your partner with thoughts of you and allowing desire for you to overwhelm all else in his/her consciousness. It is the awakening of all parts of your lover's body—not just of a select few—to ecstasy as you create a romantic mood that lasts for hours and brings you closer to a sensual feast for two. It is the door to romantic freedom that is opened through the liberating intimacy of a fantastic massage shared by two loving and caring partners who trust each other.

Sensual massage begins with understanding and joint visualization. Think of the experience as a fantasy—the opportunity to explore your lover's body with your educated hands, turning methodology into play. Turn down the lights, play some relaxing music, and talk about the day, listening to your lover's unspoken words and needs as you gently begin to massage his or her shoulders and other areas that are tense and tight. As your lover begins to relax, your minds and bodies will become one, and the journey to paradise can begin.

Eastern mystics have long claimed that our feet reflect the health of our body's various components, and that massaging the feet regularly will return the body to a state of normalization and equilibrium by combating stress through relaxation.

Sensual massages begin with the feet, freeing them from the confines of the prison cells we call shoes and allowing them to "breathe" and play. Begin by gently kneading the foot as a whole with your fingertips, exploring every nook and cranny as you rub in the soothing oil. As you feel your mate's body begin to surrender its defenses and experience the pleasure, concentrate on the toes and the pads of the feet. Move on to the depression of the arch, firmly massaging the top of the foot and bottom of the arch simultaneously, and finish with the Achilles tendon, taking your time each step of the way. After all, true relaxation comes from complete satisfaction and extended pleasure, not from rushed self-indulgence.

Begin to work your way up the back of the calf and then the thigh, spending several minutes massaging and gently kneading each muscle as you work your way to the lower back. Repeat the process two to three times, until all the tension is gone from the leg muscles of your loved one.

Continue on to the buttocks, alternating between a gentle yet firm rubbing motion with your hands, and then lightly "scratching" the derriere with your fingernails so as to enhance the sensation of the massage.

As you move up to the back, remember that it is the receptacle of all our tension—especially along the spinal cord, the body's nerve center. All our sensations, from the top of our head to the bottom of our toes, are routed through that marvelous conduit. Unfortunately, stress accumulates in the muscles that run parallel to the spine, and as these muscles become tense and put pressure on the spine, we "feel" tension, creating a mind-body connection. It is here that you need to spend the most time freeing your loved one from stress-related bonds.

Begin by generously oiling the back from the waist to the shoulder tops so that you won't have to interrupt your rhythym or break contact to apply more oil. Then, starting with the lower back, place one hand on each side of the spinal cord (with your outstretched thumbs touching) so that the base of your palms are touching the two muscular ridges on either side of the spine. Then, using plenty of pressure, move your hands upward along the back—being careful not to put pressure on the spine itself—

until you reach the shoulders. Then bring your hands back to the original position, being careful not to break contact with your loved one's body. Repeat the process several times, until you begin to feel your partner's muscles relax.

Next, moving up one side of the back, begin massaging the various muscle groups in a circular motion while applying pressure with the palms of your hands. Slowly move up the back, lingering in areas where you detect the most tension, until you reach the shoulders. Continue onto the shoulders, kneading their muscles with your hands in a circular squeezing motion for a few minutes. Then work your way down the other side of the back, in a similar fashion to the way you moved up it. Repeat the process several times by changing directions at the completion of each stroke (i.e., as you finish at the bottom of one side of the back, begin working your way back up the same side).

Finish the back massage by placing one hand on each side of the spine near the waist, with your fingertips touching. Spread your fingers and then move your hands, in opposite directions, away from the spine, applying gentle pressure. Repeat this motion, working your way up the back until you reach the shoulders.

Continue the massage by gently kneading the fleshy tissue on either side of the neck, being careful not to squeeze so hard that you hurt your loved one. Slowly work your way across the shoulders by repeatedly grasping and squeezing the muscles until you feel them begin to relax. Then continue down his/her arms (manipulating one per hand) with the same motion you used on the shoulders, until you reach your loved one's hands.

As you massage your love's hands, have him or her turn over. Then slowly massage your way back up the arms and shoulders, until you reach the head. Place your fingertips on each side of the head and gently rub the temples, using a circular motion. Then work your way down the face, caressing the facial muscles, until you reach the chest.

Work your way down by kneading the side of the body from the arm pits to the hips with your hands and thumbs and then working your way back up. After leisurely doing this several times, continue by massaging first the chest and then the abdominal muscles with the full surface of your hands, using a circular motion. Be careful not to apply too much pressure and to use extra oil.

As you work your way down to the front of his or her legs, place one hand on either side of the same leg and gently knead the muscles between your fingers and thumbs until they begin to relax. Continue doing this until you get to the ankles, and then reverse your direction. When the muscles are completely relaxed, repeat the process on the other leg.

Finish up the massage with the feet. carefully kneading and massaging them one last time. Your lover will be completely relaxed and will have thoughts only of you. Enjoy.

The effect of such a massage can be enhanced if you use hot towels. Five to ten minutes prior to giving your loved one a massage, cover her or him with several layers of dry towels, followed by several that have been placed in very hot water and wrung out. The dry towels will protect your loved one's skin from being burned, while allowing the moist heat to penetrate into the muscles. Following your massage of each area of her or his body (after removing the respective towels), cover your mate with a dry blanket or sheet that will allow the warmth of the moment to remain. Your heartthrob will be in heaven. Sensual massage is truly the ultimate aphrodisiac for two people in love!

The last twenty-five years have really made a difference in how people respond when discussing massages. Our puritanical society once considered massages to be either clinical in nature, and therefore sadomasochistic (i.e., the body had to be tortured in order to achieve good health), or an excuse to sell sex (as in massage parlors). That view has changed radically. Massages are used to both relieve pain and bring pleasure, and are offered in resorts, hotels, and health spas all over the country. What was once thought to be evil has now found a place in the center of our way of life.

An Enchanting Evening

There is a wonderful (and accurate) expression that has been around for a very long time: "The way to a man's heart is through his stomach." In truth, the adage works both ways, and for both sexes.

Everyone appreciates being pampered. It's nice to have someone take the time and make the effort to be the ultimate romantic and create a special dinner just for two. A true romantic knows that planning an elegant dinner for that very, very special someone is the pièce de résistance of romance—provided it is done with flair, class, and imagination. It is the perfect end to a loving journey filled with tender, heartfelt gestures meant to enchant.

A true romantic would begin with a love letter (or poem) inviting his or her sweetheart to share a culinary feast for two—either mailing the billet-doux or sending it by special courier (in either case with an appropriate RSVP, of course). He or she would continue to create the desired ambience, by sending either flowers or a follow-up note emphasizing how absolutely wonderful the prospect of being together seemed, knowing that this genuine and loving approach would continue to build excitement and enthusiasm.

On the intended evening, the true romantic would pick up the special guest (or, better yet, have her or him picked up, perhaps by a limousine or a horse-drawn carriage) and might have a single red rose or other appropriate gift waiting (with a glass of champagne), continuing—through such attentive, thoughtful actions—to communicate how special the loved one is.

You will find that by taking the time (and making the effort) to be creative, considerate, and loving in your approach, your evening will be a success even before dinner begins, allowing you the pleasure of your loved one's full attention and affection.

Housekeeping Notes

Nothing is more distracting to a date visiting you than laundry on the floor, an accumulation of dirty dishes in the sink, and the like. Find the time to do a thorough housecleaning well ahead of your "affair," and remember to straighten up the place, too. Buy (on the day before, if possible) everything you're going to need to make the evening an enchanting success. Work out your dinner-preparation schedule so that you can spend most of your time with your guest rather than panicking in the kitchen trying to get everything finished. (Don't forget to dress to suit the occasion and to wear an apron while tending to the cooking—but don't wear it outside the kitchen.)

Setting the Mood

If you want to have an especially elegant evening, you may wish to hire a maître d' to serve your gourmet fare with class and distinction, freeing your time so you can concentrate on your guest. You may even want to hire a pianist or violinist to add that extra touch of sophistication. The main thing to remember is that since this evening is dedicated to the one you love, it should be creatively and lovingly planned around her or his needs, desires, and joys—not yours.

The Table

Since quite a bit of your evening is going to be spent at your dining room table, you need to make a special effort to ensure that the message it sends is consistent with the rest of your efforts.

It needs to be set according to both the menu you have selected and your loved one's preferences, making sure that you have all the appropriate china, silverware, goblets, napkins, serving pieces, and decorations to make that special person feel wonderfully spoiled. Decorate simply but elegantly. (After all, elegance is the key to a truly romantic dinner.) Candles, flowers, and a "scroll" with the menu on it wrapped with a ribbon (the ultimate in class) can be attractive and inventive finishing touches. If you have taken the time to "do it right," love might just blossom all around you, lifting passion to new heights.

The Menu

You should plan gourmet delights that are designed to enchant the man or woman you love, surprising him or her with your exquisite taste, proving amazing with your culinary talents, and showing a sensitive side of yourself that brings your sweetheart a sense of wonderment and joy.

Begin by selecting your menu. Since you are planning a dinner, will you be serving a salad, soup, or another appetizer? What will the main course be? What kind of side dishes (vegetables, rolls…) will be presented with the entree? Do you plan on serving dessert? What kinds of drinks (aperitifs, water, wine, coffee, etc.) will you offer with your meal?

Once you have done this and are comfortable with your selection (i.e., that the foods chosen will in combination taste "right" as well as look good together), make a shopping list of all the necessities. It will keep you from accidentally forgetting to pick up something you need. Don't leave home without it!

Next, determine when you would like each course served—and, using the instructions in your cookbook, work your way backward, creating a recipe for the whole meal. In other words, think of the time you want to serve your last course as "zero hour" and select what needs to be done fifteen minutes, thirty minutes, forty-five minutes, an hour, an hour and a half, or even thirty-six hours before. Develop this "guide" and follow it, and any meal you plan will (with any luck at all) come out both perfect and on time.

One final suggestion: When serving follow-up dinners (or other meals), experiment—try things you've been thinking you can't make. By taking advantage of a good cookbook and careful preparation, you will surprise yourself—and please yur lover immensely.

Bon appetit!

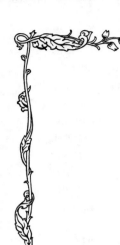

Wine for Romantic Occasions

or thousands of years, connoisseurs from all over the world have considered wine ("the nectar of the gods and lovers") to be the perfect complement to any occasion, whether it be a celebration, a picnic on the beach, or an elegant dinner. But it has only been since the 1960s that we have really become a nation of wine *drinkers*, enjoying more copiously the wonderful benefits of the grape—savoring its enchanting taste and bouquet, and making it part of not only our everyday life but also our love life.

Today, most Americans feel somewhat confused by the number of wines available to them and so believe that it is sometimes difficult to choose the right one for each occasion. In fact, one of the many nice things about wine is that there are a great many "right" choices among them and very few "wrong" ones.

Conventional wisdom (before Americans began to truly appreciate wine) held that there were three rules that were gospel. The first was that white wine is to be served with white meat, and red wine with red meat. However, since cooking styles as well as tastes have "matured" over the last few years, today the rule of thumb is that every situation needs to be dealt with separately. Factors such as the overall menu, how the food is cooked (for instance, is it a white meat cooked in a red wine sauce?), the

"The wine-cup is glad! Dear Oenophile's lip
It boasts to have touched when she stooped down to sip.
Happy wine-cup! I wish that, with lips joined to mine,
All my soul at a draught she would drink up like wine."
—ACILIUS

time of day, the setting, the company, and the weather all are important considerations that need to be part of your decision. In fact, each time you serve the same entree, the appropriate wine selection may change. For example: If you were to serve chicken cacciatore (chicken in a red wine sauce) for lunch on a Sunday in the summer, the perfect selection would be a California Johannesburg Riesling (an off-dry white wine). The identical meal served as a dinner for friends might call for a French Beaujolais (a red wine). However, if you served your repast in an intimate setting to someone very special, a California Reserve Cabernet Sauvignon (semi-dry red wine), or a Grand Cru red wine fron the Bordeaux region of France would be appropriate. Here you have the same menu with a choice of three different wines—all of which would be correct.

The second piece of conventional wisdom (no longer considered gospel, but still a very good guideline) is that—when comparing wines—the costs of the bottles, corks, labels, and associated fees usually are about on a par. (This assumed that you were comparing similar products—e.g., California Chardonnays to the same, and German Liebfraumilches ditto.) So the difference in cost was then, and still usually is, about equal to the difference in quality. Your challenge, if you want the most for your money, is to sample until you find what you consider the best buys available. As you drink a wine, make a mental (or real) note of the label and of what you like and don't like about what's the bottle. Simply put, experience still is the best teacher of taste.

The final great truth (which has not changed) is very simple: Wine, like food and love, is one of life's great pleasures—especially when enjoyed with someone special. When you find a wine you both like, sharing it can be pure poetry.

The nicest thing about wine is that there are so many choices—not just of reds

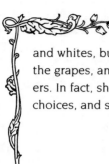

and whites, but of varieties from different grapes, soils, weather, methods of growing the grapes, and—most important, the skills of (and equipment used by) the winemakers. In fact, shopping for wine is a lot like being in a candy store: so many wonderful choices, and so little time to enjoy them all. But what a way to live!

Dionysus, the youngest son of Zeus (the chief god on Olympus), was conceived when Zeus appeared to Semele, a mortal princess, in disguise and made love to her. Shortly after this, Zeus's wife, Hera, Goddess of Marriage, learned of the liaison and, in a fit of jealousy, went to Semele, telling her the truth about Zeus. She persuaded the innocent Semele to ask Zeus to visit her again, but this time as himself. Unable to refuse this request, Zeus complied. As a result, Semele was consumed by the fire of his radiance. Hermes, another of Zeus's sons (who was born as the result of an affair with the goddess Maia), learned of Hera's intention to destroy the mother and baby and saved Dionysus by removing him from his mother's womb just before she died and sewing him into Zeus's leg. After Dionysus was born, Hermes continued to protect him from Hera by hiding him in a valley, where he was raised by nymphs. It was there that he discovered grapes and invented the winemaking process, becoming the God of Wine and one of the most beloved mythical figures of all time.

If you would really like to share a romantic moment with your loved one, serve peaches with your wine, or strawberries with your champagne, and feed each other. This will prove to be a truly delicious time spent together.

Love Potions

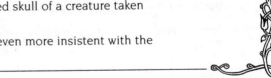

The quest for the ultimate love potion (they also were known as *philtres* and *magic potions*) is as old as civilization itself.

The ancient Greeks and Romans used a variety of both exotic and potentially dangerous ingredients in their efforts to brew the perfect concoction that would induce amorous feelings in their loved ones. Some were highly successful, while others proved deadly. In spite of the danger, however, these potions were so prevalent in both societies that a number of historians, including Horace, wrote of them often, and imperial decrees were occasionally issued limiting their sale.

Some of the more popular ingredients used in these philtres, according to the historian Plutarch, included animal secretions and excrement; semen; various organs (including sexual ones) of certain land animals and birds; bones of frogs; and parts of any plant, shrub, or tree that was thought to have aphrodisiacal effects—such as betel-tree nuts, mandrake roots, and tobacco leaves. The poet Propertius added to this list by referring to a potion made from snake bones, frogs, and owl feathers; and the novelist Apuleius further added the powdered skull of a creature taken from the jaws of a dangerous wild animal.

The demand for love potions became even more insistent with the

advent of the Middle Ages. A great many European ballads, legends, and sagas sung and told even today speak of the wondrous powers of these potions. In fact, regions of Europe still exist where potions continue to be made from recipes passed from generation to generation via such stories.

This fascination with love potions has transcended geographic, cultural, and religious boundaries. Some of the more popular brews used during the past few centuries have included almond nectar (using raw almonds and honey, as recommended by sixteenth-century Arabs), Angel Water (a popular eighteenth-century Portuguese drink made of orange-flower water, rose water, myrtle water, distilled spirit of musk, and spirit of ambergris), aphrodisiac wine (an Italian recipe of cinnamon, ginger, rhubarb, vanilla, and wine), and bird's nest soup (a Chinese preparation made from the nests of sea swallows that is reputed to be highly effective in inducing amorous feelings).

Even Shakespeare was seduced by the belief in philtres. In *Macbeth* he devoted a scene to the creation of a magic potion, and in A *Midsummer Night's Dream* described another to be used on Titania.

Love potions still exist, albeit in different forms. Acceptance of long-term monogamous relationships, concern for our loved one's health and well-being, and a better understanding of the laws of attraction all have changed our perceptions of what is acceptable—and even necessary—in a philtre. Love has become its own philtre, and romance the main ingredient.

Modern love potions (usually but not always of the alcholic kind) often reflect each user couple's combined personality and desire, enhancing their amorous feelings by means of a liquid libation that is exquisite in taste to both and which releases their inhibitions, allowing them to explore in more uninhibited ways than usual their feelings for one another.

Although there's a wide variety of modern love potions available to choose from, some of the more popular include the following. We'll call them our Top Ten—but it'll be up to you to try them and decide in which order they *should* be listed.

Love Potion No. 1—"Spiritual Seduction"

Serve chilled French champagne (or Italian Asti Spumante) with strawberries.

Love Potion No. 2—_Variation on a Theme by_ "B&B"

Carefully blend one ounce each of Benedictine and fine French cognac, and serve over ice in a snifter large enough for two to share.

Love Potion No. 3—"_Lover's Delight_"

Make a large chocolate malt (with real chocolate) and serve complete with two long straws.

Love Potion No. 4—"_The Love Potion_"

The initial ingredients (a blend of three ounces of cognac, one and a half ounces of lemon juice, one ounce of apricot brandy, and half an ounce of maraschino liqueur poured over several slices of fresh, ripe pineapple covered with half a cup of sugar) should be allowed to marinate, covered, overnight. The love potion itself is perfected by pouring the marinade over ice in a small punchbowl (preferably a size perfect for two), blending in a bottle of champagne, and serving it all with fresh slices of oranges and lemons—and, of course, two straws.

Love Potion No. 5—"_Chocolate Coffee à l'Amour_"

Melt (don't burn) one ounce of sweet white chocolate in a double boiler. Add half a cup of sugar, a pinch of salt, and one and three-quarter cups of water to the melted chocolate. Beat the contents with a whisk (or some such) until the mixture is smooth, and allow it to simmer for five minutes. Add half a cup each of milk and light cream, and reheat the potion until it is warm but not near bubbling, stirring occasionally. Add one teaspoon of vanilla, one ounce of amaretto, one ounce of cognac, and two cups of freshly made hot coffee, and beat it all again. Serve the love potion over a scoop of French vanilla ice cream in an oversized coffee cup.

Love Potion No. 6—"_Café Royale_"

Since both taste and presentation are essential to the success of this love potion, it should be prepared in the presence of your loved one. Pour your mate a cup of very hot coffee. Then place a cube (or the equivalent amount) of sugar in a tablespoon

filled with warm cognac, and slowly lower the spoon into the cup _but not yet into the coffee._ When the mix ignites, then carefully flow it onto the surface of the coffee. After your loved one has been dazzled by this splendid sight, have her or him stir the concoction— and enjoy a very special love potion that will lower inhibitions while invigorating that body you so admire.

Love Potion No. 7—"Angel's Dream"

Fill two liqueur glasses three-quarters full of apricot brandy (reputed to be a highly effective aphrodisiac) and top them off with heavy cream.

Love Potion No. 8—"Chartreuse Champagne Cocktail"

Place a teaspoon of sugar, two drops of Angostura bitters, and two teaspoons of cognac into each of two tall champagne glasses. Allow the mixture to marinate for a little while, then fill each with chilled champagne—leaving just enough room at the top to float a teaspoon of Chartreuse on top. Besides being a wonderful drink, this is a delight to behold.

Love Potion No. 9—"Between the Sheets"

Half fill a cocktail shaker with ice. Add two ounces each of Bacardi light rum, cognac and Cointreau, plus the juice of a lemon, and shake vigorously. Strain the love potion into two chilled glasses and serve. The name says it all.

Love Potion No. 10—"Cherry Celebration"

Pour three ounces of cherry juice, eight ounces of Sprite, and a dash of Angostura bitters into a cocktail shaker half filled with ice. Add the juice of a lime, and an ounce of bar syrup. Shake the love potion vigorously and then strain it into two highball glasses containing ice cubes and cherries. Enjoy!

Love potions are simply meant to be a "fun" way to enhance the feelings that two lovers already share—love, trust, caring, and friendship. It is these feelings, and their accompanying desire, that more than anything else make a love potion effective.

"I will show you a philtre without potions, without herbs, without any witch's incantation: if you wish to be loved, love."
—Seneca

One of the most famous love potions in literature was the one written about by Shakespeare in his Midsummer Night's Dream:

OBERON:
That very time I saw, but thou couldst not,
Flying between the cold moon and the earth,
Cupid all arm'd: a certain aim he took
At a fair vestal throned by the west,
And loosed his love-shaft smartly from his bow,
As it should pierce a hundred thousand hearts:
But I might see young Cupid's fiery shaft
Quench'd in the chaste beams of the watery moon,
And the imperial voltaress passed on,
In maiden meditation, fancy-free.
Yet mark'd I where the bolt of Cupid fell:
It fell upon a little western flower,
Before milk-white, now purple with love's wound,
And maidens call it love-in-idleness.
Fetch me that flower; the herb I shew'd thee once:
The juice of it on sleeping eyelids laid
Will make man or woman madly dote
Upon the next live creature that it sees.

Fetch me this herb; and be thou here again
Ere the leviathan can swim a league.

PUCK:
I'll put a girdle round about the earth
In forty minutes.

OBERON:
Having once this juice,
I'll watch Titania when she is asleep,
And drop the liquor of it in her eyes.
The next thing then she waking looks upon,
Be it lion, bear, or wolf, or bull,
On meddling monkey, or on busy ape,
She shall pursue it with the soul of love:
And ere I take this charm off from her sight,
As I can take it with another herb,
I'll make her render up her page to me.

Heavenly Love

Throughout history a great many people have believed that our lives are ruled by the ever-changing yet always constant position and movements of the sun and the solar system's planets, and that each of us has our own very specific horoscope and destiny.

While not everyone agrees with this view, the incontrovertible fact is that astrology *is* interesting. We all, at one time or another, have enjoyed reading the general horoscopes in the newspapers and magazines. Some of us have taken them seriously, others have laughed, and many of us have expressed an internal desire to learn more about this fascinating subject.

Perhaps the most appealing thing about the zodiac and all that it portends is that studying it allows us the opportunity for self-discovery and change. Most of the generalized descriptions (variations do exist as a result of our Ascendant or Moon sign, and due to the influences of heredity) seem—even to "doubters"—to be fairly accurate overall. By recognizing the traits, both positive and negative, that make up the personality of each of us, we come ever closer both to self-acceptance and to the realization that there may be changes we each need to make in our personalities and personal lives alike in order to have a more fulfilling relationship with the one (and the ones) we love. After all, the ability to love comes from learning to love *ourselves*!

The following is a brief rundown of characteristics generally typical of those born under each of the twelve signs of the zodiac. As you read them, think of people you know whose birthdays fall somewhere within the time limits specified, and see whether these "fit" them.

Aries (the Ram)

The first sign of the zodiac (and the first Fire sign), Aries (March 21 to April 19), is ruled by Mars, the God of War, and begins with the first day of Spring. (The zodiacal year is not the *calendar* year, but rather a *seasonal* year. The order of signs, month by month each quarter, is akin to the natural development of Earth's formation: Fire to Earth, then Air to Water—or, in other words, from insubstantial to substantial.)

Aries men love to be in love—constantly looking for that perfect mate, showering her with lavish affection and attention. They have an idealistic view of life, believing that one day they will find their own special someone who will love them completely and faithfully and will never let them down. While they may seem egotistical, bossy, and impatient at times, they always make life interesting for their partner—as well as everyone else around

Aries women are tough, aggressive, impulsive, headstrong individuals who love their independence yet can be the most loving of partners *if* they trust and respect their mate. Passionate, emotional, loyal, and adventurous, they bring excitement to a relationship. Simply put, an Aries woman is a feminine feminist who believes that *anything* is possible, both in love and in life.

Taurus (the Bull)

The second sign of the zodiac, Venus-ruled Taurus (April 20 to May 20), is one of its most sensual (although this isn't always apparent, since Taureans rarely rush into relationships). It is an Earth sign.

Taurus men tend to be strong, dependable individuals who think everything through before they make decisions. They value loyalty and security above all else and can be somewhat obstinate when pushed. However, once they have chosen their mate, they are extremely romantic, patient, understanding, caring, and easygoing, wanting only to make her happy.

Despite the fact that the Taurus woman was born under a a feminine sign ruled by Venus, the Goddess of Love, they are anything but submissive—although they are willing to take second place _if_ they love and respect their mate. Like their male counterparts, Taurus women are slow to get involved, but once they do, they do so with a long-term relationship in mind. Virtuous, loyal, practical, intuitive, and sensual, they make ideal mates (especially to someone willing to treat them as their equal, and who can get past their inherent stubbornness). Loving and dependable, they become their mate's best friend, greatest lover, and most devoted supporter.

Gemini (the Twins)

Gemini (May 21 to June 21) is ruled by Mercury, the planet of communication, and is an Air sign.

Gemini men tend to be irresistible charmers who have a need for constant change and variety in their lives. They are known as the social butterflies of the zodiac, although deep down they are looking for someone to love who will accept them as they are. Moody, bossy, demanding, and unpredictable, Gemini men also are (strange to say) romantic, interesting, intellectually stimulating, and willing to communicate their feelings. As they mature, Gemini men make excellent love mates.

Gemini women tend to be two (or more) people in one body, as shown by the sign of the twins and evidenced by their myriad moods and easily bored nature. They have a great need to communicate their thoughts and feelings, and want to be appreciated for both their mind and their body. While Gemini women find it difficult to settle down with one man, they do believe in true love, and would enhance the life of any man they fell in love with. Wanting to neither dominate or be dominated in a relationship, Gemini women are fascinating, inspirational individuals who will help a relationship reach heights seldom dreamed of when with the right lover.

Cancer (the Crab)

Ruled by the Moon, Cancer (June 22 to July 22) is the first of the Water signs.

Cancer men are leaders at heart. Their personalities are controlled by their emotions, and because of this they can be very tender and compassionate. They are extremely family-oriented and want a stable, secure, loving relationship. They tend to

be romantic idealists (albeit with a practical streak) who want permanence in their lives. While they can be opinionated, argumentative, and moody, they nevertheless are perceptive and kind, understanding the value of love and affection.

Although Cancer women thrive on having loving families, they are definitely not dependent little housewives. They can be highly emotional, bossy, and moody—yet they more often than not are warm, caring, loyal, sensitive individuals who want to create the perfect life for the man they love. Desirous of a long-term, secure relationship because of their belief in living happily ever after, Cancer women have traditional, conservative family values and make wonderful love mates.

Leo (the Lion)

Ruled by the Sun, Leo (July 23 to August 22) is the regal ruler of the zodiac. It is a Fire sign.

Since Leo rules the heart, Leo men seek love in their lives. Hopeless romantics, they usually are enthusiastic, devoted, warm, loving partners with hearts of gold. Born to be leaders, they can have a stubborn and opinionated nature but don't like being surrounded by "yes" people—especially in marriage. They love to be respected and in turn surround themselves with people they respect. Leo men are both very personable and magnanimous by nature, and are the world's eternal optimists, believing that everything is possible and that there is great goodness in human nature.

Leo women are bright-shining stars who enjoy being the center of attention and need a lot of love in their lives. While they may seem forceful, independent, and even bossy, Leo women are creative, vital, and loving. When they meet someone they can admire and respect, they become more like pussycats than lionesses, willing to share the limelight with the men they love. They have warm dispositions, are incurable optimists, are very generous and extremely passionate, and can brighten up the life of any man lucky enough to be part of their lives—*provided* he allows them their independence and gives them the respect they deserve.

Virgo (the Virgin)

Ruled by Mercury, the planet of communication, Virgo (August 23 to September 22) is known as the sign of service and is an Earth sign.

Virgo men tend to be perfectionists. Honest and direct, they tend to worry a lot, especially about money and security. However, they *can* be the best choice for a partner. Virgo men want a permanent relationship in their lives but are slow to commit until they have evaluated all aspects of the relationship. Once committed, however, they love with devoted passion, knowing that they don't often make mistakes and that their true love is the love of their life.

Virgo women also seek perfection in their lives. Pure of heart, loving, caring, hardworking, and filled with a strong sense of duty, they want permanence in their lives. They are very adept at expressing their feelings, and extremely rational in their approach to life and love. They like to be friends before becoming lovers—but, once committed, become very loyal, loving partners.

Libra (the Balance)

Ruled by Venus, the Goddess of Love, Libra (September 23 to October 22) is the sign of the Scales, signifying peace and harmony. It is an Air sign.

Libra men are sensitive yet very strong, charming, diplomatic, and a genuine pleasure to be with. Great at communicating ideas, they are fairly irresistible even though they have a well-earned reputation for indecision and extravagance. However, while they certainly are cautious about making most decisions, carefully weighing every last possibility before coming to a conclusion, they are firmly ruled by Venus—and so have been known to rush headlong into a relationship. Their perhaps greatest quandary arises when they feel that they may have made a mistake of the heart and aren't sure how to tell their partner so without hurting her feelings. (One of the most important things to remember about single Libra men is that they are searching for the *perfect* partner.) Once truly paired off, they settle down with assurance to be kind, loving, gentle, understanding, and devoted partners.

Being in love is what it's all about for Libra women. Bright, witty, affectionate, kind, and extremely feminine, Libra women are nevertheless slow in making decisions, especially when it comes to long-term relationships. Their greatest desire is to attract a partner to share their lives with, in order to find happiness as part of a team. Once they have decided that they've found the perfect man, they give the relationship everything they have to offer. This does *not* mean that they're willing to give up their own dreams

and aspirations, however. It *does* mean that they'll help their partner to reach his goals but will expect the same consideration in return. Simply put, Libra women are a perfect mixture of masculine strengths and feminine sensitivities, far more often than not bringing peace and harmony into the lives of the one they love, while constantly stimulating him mentally and emotionally.

Scorpio (the Scorpion)

Ruled by two planets—Mars (God of War) and Pluto (Lord of the Underword)—Scorpio (October 23 to November 21) is a Water sign.

If there is one word that best describes the Scorpio male, it is *invincible*. His inner strength, magnetic personality, and powerful ego allow the woman he is with to feel protected and secure. Passionately intense about sex, Scorpio men have a reputation for being the sex symbols of the zodiac, genuinely enjoying involvement in sexual relationships. However, they are equally interested in the mind (they have an insatiable curiosity), so can be great partners in a long-term relationship when both these needs are met. Willing to do anything to win the affection of someone they care about, Scorpio men are very self-confident. And they usually are extremely loyal to their mate.

Having been born under an extremely amorous sign, Scorpio women tend to be extremely sensual. (It goes without saying tht they *also* are invincible.) Highly sensitive by nature, they have a strong depth of emotions, display unusual psychic abilities, and value (and guard) their privacy. Once a Scorpio woman feels she has met the man of her dreams (being to some extent psychic, she usually "knows" when he is right), she will work at building a perfect life with him. While forgiveness does not come easily to these women, they tend to be loyal to, and dependable toward, those they care about.

Saggitarius (the Archer)

Ruled by Jupiter, planet of good fortune, Sagittarius (November 22 to December 21) is a Fire sign. It is known as the explorer of the zodiac.

Born with insatiable curiosity, Sagittarius males are usually lovable, happy-go-lucky individuals who are highly restless by nature. They can have a delightful personality and sense of humor and are equally at ease with comedy and philosophy. Incredibly optimistic, they seem to love everyone, and everyone seems to love them back. They are very self-confident and honest, so of course love to give advice. While their wanderlust can be a bit disconcerting to some women, Sagittarius males make great long-term partners, bringing untold depths to the relationship—especially with a partner who likes to be independent and respected in her own right. In fact, Sagittarius men become both wonderful lovers and best friends with their partners because of their wonderfully supportive, giving natures.

Sagittarius women have total, unshakable faith in themselves, and because of this are incredible optimists. Independent and strong-willed, they are inclined to tackle any situation that comes their way, cheerfully accepting the risks that may be involved, and have a zest for life second to none. They are bright and warm-hearted and always have a great many friends because of their receptive and interesting personalities. Open and honest in relationships, they make life with them pure pleasure. They are loyal, loving, and lovable!

Capricorn (the Goat)

Ruled by Saturn, taskmaster of the Zodiac, Capricorn (December 21 to January 19) is an Earth sign.

Capricorn men are natural leaders who exemplify persistence and determination. They are reliable, security-oriented (especially where material success is concerned), and conscious of the need for satisfying their loved one's emotional needs. For the most part, they make devoted, considerate partners who believe in tradition and conformity and take their responsibilities seriously. Although their extremely practical natures prevent them from making romantic commitments too quickly, once committed, they become the ultimate partner.

Capricorn women have a strength and determination about them that scare some men but allow the women to make it past everything that life puts in their way. Careful by nature, they don't rush into relationships, no matter *how* attractive they find someone, preferring instead to get to know that person better first. Their deep-seated belief in the sanctity of marriage and the importance of long-term relationships, as well as their high moral standards, make them incredibly devoted, loving partners. They are practical, hard-working, and extremely well organized individuals who have a firm grip on their priorities. Once committed to a relationship, they are wonderful mates.

Aquarius (the Water Bearer)

Ruled by Uranus, planet of change, invention, and disruption, Aquarius (January 20 to February 18) is an Air sign. It was also the most celebrated sign of the sixties, the age of Aquarius.

Aquarius men do not like to follow in anyone else's footsteps, instead preferring to choose their own path, one that exemplifies their personal ideals and visions of a better world. The words that best describe them are *original*, *unpredictable*, and *unconventional*. Completely individualistic, they make wonderful friends and are brilliant conversationalists on a platonic level. Unfortunately, them seem to find communication on a one-on-one level difficult, making them appear cold and uncaring, no matter how strongly they feel. Because of this, Aquarius men are inclined to prefer getting to know their partners as friends before they become their lovers. Highly intelligent, perceptive, creative, and intuitive, they love their personal sense of freedom. They can also be somewhat moody. Once committed to a relationship (especially if they spent a considerable amout of time getting to that point), Aquarius men work hard at making it a success and are truly devoted partners.

Aquarius women tend to be extremely elusive and individualistic—rebels against convention. Free-spirited, honest, understanding, intuitive, tolerant, and supportive, they make wonderful friends but (like their male counterparts of this sign) are slow to form long-term love relationships. They constantly explore new ideas and add exhilaration to the lives of the people they touch. Most of all, they are romantic idealists with a personal vision of how to make the world a better place to live in.

Pisces (the Fishes)

The romantic dreamer of the zodiac, Pisces (February 19 to March 20) is ruled by Neptune, the planet of inspiration and illusion. In many ways the consummate birth sign, the symbol of Pisces is of two fish, one swimming upstream and the other downstream, signifying the quality of their nature. Pisces is also the last of the water signs, making those born under this birth sign receptive to outside influences

Pisces men love romance and chasing romantic dreams. They look at life though rose-colored glasses, believing that everything is possible, even if their dreams are sometimes unrealistic and impractical. Sensitive, intuitive, compassionate, and emotional, Pisces men live for romance (believing it to be one of the great necessities of life) and will do anything for the one they love. Bringing magic to the sexual side of any long-term relationship, they love to make love to the person they have chosen to spend their life with.

Pisces women are the most romantic in the whole zodiac. Feminine beyond belief, they live for romance, love, and "living happily ever after." Much like their male counterparts, Pisces women have a very rosy outlook on life and are creative and artistic in their approach to it. They tend to be wise, wonderful lovers intent on making their partners happy, and have well-earned reputations of being soft, sensitive, and compassionate.

Beautiful Dreamer

reams reflect our most intimate experiences. They are a daily "concentration" of our subjective thoughts and feelings and seem to transcend the barriers of time past, present, and future. It is through our dreams that we create a personal world view that gives us the ability to understand our future. A view that warns us of danger and heralds joy and happiness.

Dreams, which are visual in nature, image every unseen emotion we can only feel, profoundly affecting us with their dynamic forcefulness. They can be happy, sad, reassuring, frightening, inspirational, sexual, religious, entertaining—and every other possibility from among the range of ways we respond to events in our lives.

It would be safe to say that fascination with dreams (and of course their interpretations) is as old as human life itself, having apparently been found, for example, recorded on cave walls. In fact, the subject of dreams was of such great interest to the Assyrians, Babylonians, and Egyptians that books on dreams were available to them, as they were in just about every language of early recorded history, including Greek, Latin, Hebrew, and Arabic.

Today we enjoy the best understanding of dreams, ever, thanks to the

mountain of research on this fascinating subject, as well as the advent of modern equipment to help measure and analyze our dreams.

Not only do we all dream, but *nothing is impossible in a dream*. In fact, we have a minimum of three dreams a night and can have as many as nine, and *each* is a private play produced and directed using our very own script, and viewed by a private audience of one.

Many of our dreams have no real subconscious or clairvoyant significance, since they can be traced to some physical or psychological cause, such as background noises that don't completely awaken us but register as part of our dream; grieving over the loss of someone special; or the consumption of too much food or alcohol just before going to bed, to name a few. However, we all have dreams—usually between 2 a.m. and 7 a.m.—that fall into the precognitive, warning, factual, and inspirational categories. Among these are dreams that foretell future events in our lives, suggest impending danger, confirm something we believe to be true, or offer solutions to our personal challenges—especially in such important areas as our love life.
Do you know that some authorities on the subject believe that:

♥ Dreaming about anything abnormal (such as a horse with feathers) can mean you will soon have an acceptable solution to a pressing problem.

♥ A dream about having a lot of things in abundance is a good omen.

♥ To see an acacia in bloom in a dream is a promising augur of your most secret passions.

♥ A dream involving the Ace, King, Queen, or Jack of Hearts signifies success in love.

♥ If you dream about achievement, the greater the achievement, the greater the satisfaction coming your way.

♥ Acorns and the trees that bear them predict prosperity and good fortune in a dream.

♥ A dream involving the adoration of someone special is the forerunner to deep peace and contentment.

♥ Dreams involving affection indicate happy personal relationships.

♥ To smell, taste, or use allspice in a dream is considered to be a wonderful romantic omen.

♥ To have amorous feelings toward someone you know while dreaming suggests that the relationship could ripen into romance.

♥ If you dream about an aquamarine, you will have a very happy love life.

♥ Your love life will improve if you dream about avocados.

♥ Dreams about baboons portend a happy marriage.

♥ There will be love, happiness, and prosperity in your life if you dream of an elegant banquet.

♥ A dream of beauty forecasts success in romantic love.

♥ Dreaming of butterflies signifies romantic success.

♥ There will be love, happiness, respect, and prosperity in your life if you dream about a carpenter.

♥ Eating dates in a dream predicts an upcoming marriage.

♥ A dream involving white doves promises a happy home life.

♥ Long, beautiful eyelashes in a dream predict romantic bliss.

♥ Dreams about freckles (yours or someone else's) promise popularity with members of the opposite sex.

♥ Dreaming about gardenias promises an upcoming love affair.

♥ A greenhouse in a dream portends a bright future full of love.

♥ Dreams of harems signify busy times ahead with the opposite sex.

♥ Seeing something heart-shaped (such as a picture frame) in a dream promises a happy, romantic relationship.

♥ Watching someone perform the hula in your dreams forecasts an exciting, romantic adventure.

♥ Dreams involving kissing someone you like predict happiness and contentment.

♥ A dream of lace, or clothes made with lace, promises great success in the area of romance.

♥ Seeing a lighthouse at night in your dreams is a sign of good fortune in love.

♥ Dreams of sincere love are a forecast of happiness in your future.

♥ Dreaming of a magnet predicts popularity with members of the opposite sex.

♥ The smell of musk in your dream could lead to a passionate romantic affair in the near future.

♥ Wearing or owning a beautiful necklace in a dream usually promises a life filled with romance and love.

♥ A dream involving a nymph forecasts an upcoming romantic liaison.

♥ Using a parachute (successfully) in a dream portends a happy love life.

♥ Dreams about pumpkins promise a happy home life.

♥ A dream about a rainbow predicts upcoming happiness.

♥ Gathering fresh roses in your dream is a forecast of joy to come.

♥ A happy love affair could be the result of wearing a bright scarf in a dream.

♥ Smelling scented soap in a dream signifies your enjoyment of, and satisfaction with, an ongoing romantic involvement.

♥ Using a spear in a dream promises an exciting love affair in your future.

♥ Strawberries represent upcoming happiness when they are part of a dream.

♥ Dreaming of eating a sundae in a dream promises success with the opposite sex.

♥ A happy homelife full of love is predicted by a dream involving a thimble.

♥ A dream featuring wine served in a glass promises happiness, good health, and prosperity.

So—if you are a woman and dream of picking roses in the presence of a rainbow while wearing a bright scarf and a beautiful necklace, or if you are a man and dream of kissing your loved one shortly after you share a glass of wine and strawberries with her, then you will have a long and happy love life ahead of you!

"Unimaginative people dream in black and white, but poets dream in glorious color."
—ANONYMOUS

Romantic Dates for Two

he key to successful romance is spending quality time together, doing things you both enjoy. One of the best things about romance is that it doesn't necessarily have to cost a lot of money all the time. Indeed, the recipe for a great "fun" date often may require only three ingredients: you, your loved one, and a little prior planning. Naturally, every time you add to the recipe, you're bound to incur additional outlays—so plan *wisely*.

Here are fifteen suggestions for fun dates, beginning with the *least* expensive.

♥ Go for a romantic walk. This is a wonderful way to share both precious time and loving thoughts, and can be the greatest date of all.

♥ Take an evening swim together. It can be a very sensual experience!

♥ Try star-gazing in a canoe or rowboat one evening. (Or, during the day, make it eye-gazing.)

♥ Visit a playground and take turns pushing and sitting on a swing, or riding side-by-side, listening to each other's dreams, aspirations, and needs and bringing back memories of a time when life was much sim-

pler and more carefree. This is especially nice to do on an the evening when the stars are out.

♥ Share breakfast at a romantic restaurant, sipping coffee together, starting each other's morning off on a very romantic note, and leaving each other with thoughts of the evening to come.

♥ Surprise your love by fixing a picnic lunch or dinner and going together to a scenic park to enjoy it, complete with your favorite drinks, and candles for a touch of romantic class. Or take a small table and set up dinner on the beach (complete with white or checkered tablecloth, depending on your mood). Enjoy luxurious moments of peace and quiet set in nature's paradise for two.

♥ Escape to a romantic hideaway for an evening of dancing. Become as one as you move in rhythm to music that captures your imagination. Feel the heat of your bodies fuel the passion of your souls. Sense the promise of ardor to come.

♥ Create an in-house dining experience that he or she won't forget. For instance, tell your loved one that the two of you are going to have dinner on a gondola in Venice— then pull a surprise by simulating the experience. All it takes is a few stage props that can be made from cardboard and other materials, the right lighting, the proper music, and of course a menu and wine appropriate to the occasion. Besides having fun, you will both have a repast to remember—and, with any luck at all, the rest of the night with it. (This could even work as a dinner on the bay, viewing San Francisco's skyline, or in Paris, marveling at the Eiffel Tower, or—use your imagination.)

♥ Request dinner out—and do it in style. Ask her or him for a date, via flowers or a love letter delivered by someone dressed in a tuxedo or formal gown (respectively, of course). Don't forget the RSVP card!

♥ Find out when his or her favorite singer, group, play, opera, or whatever is going to be in town (or nearby), get two of the best tickets to the right performance, and *go*.

♥ Treat her or him to a surprise weekend at a local hotel, and when there forget about everything except each other.

♥ Indulge your loved one's favorite pastime (skiing, golf, fashion show, ballet, ball game) in a special way by making arrangements to enjoy it *together*.

♥ Enjoy a romantic ride with your love in a hot-air balloon, soaring through the heavens, free as birds.

♥ Ski together during a winter weekend at a romantic resort. (*Learn* to ski together if you don't already know how to.) During the summer spend a weekend at a dude ranch where you can go hiking, horseback riding, on hayrides, to barn dances, and so on. (Riding and dancing lessons usually are available. Hiking and hayrides come naturally.)

♥ Plan a trip with your lover to some famous city that has a reputation for being genuinely romantic. Figure on staying long enough to find out for yourselves. The local convention and visitors' bureau or chamber of commerce there (if not one in your own area) can help you finalize your travel plans and make solid suggestions about events you might like to attend and accommodations and entertainment you could take advantage of. Newspapers (usually the Thursday or Friday editions), local magazines, and friends also are great sources of ideas for romantic dates.

Put some thought into whatever you intend to do together—and (whatever it is) enjoy each other while doing it!

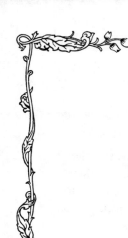

Romantic Dates Extraordinaire

ave you ever wanted to do something special with your loved one that was more than a date but less than a vacation? Something truly special? Something in fact extraordinary? If you have, the good news is that the extraordinary takes just a little longer than the ordinary—a little longer to plan, a little longer to save up for, and a little longer to enjoy. But the benefits are fabulous: There's time to yourselves—away from the telephone, the neighbors, the boss, and the kids. There's the freedom to share an exotic and memorable experience and leave the reminders of a more settled lifestyle behind (if only for a few days). And there's the pleasure of simply being together and having fun.

Every couple has their own definition of the kind of romantic experience that would qualify as a romantic date extraordinaire. And while the content will vary from couple to couple, the essence of the idea always remains the same—two to four days of doing something very, very special, away from the everyday confines of day-to-day life.

Some couples might enjoy flying into New York City for dinner at a Five Star restaurant, a show on Broadway, or a concert at Carnegie Hall— and in any case also a tour of the Big Apple.

Other couples might prefer spending two to three days in New Orleans during Jazzfest in April; or in San Francisco and the nearby wine

country; or in Las Vegas, watching the lavish shows; or in Boston, listening to the Boston Pops and eating fresh lobster; or in Washington, D.C., visiting the monuments and cultural centers. There is something special for everyone to see or do in (or near) just about every major city in the United States.

Couples who enjoy a quieter lifestyle might enjoy a weekend cruise for two or staying at a luxury hotel in some exotic locale like Mazatlán, the Bahamas, or the Pocono Mountains that caters to lovers. They might even enjoy (and prefer) spending a few days alone in a private shady cabin in the mountains or in a sunny house on the beach.

Sports enthusiasts could turn the Olympics, the World Series, the Superbowl, the U.S. Open, and any number of other premier sporting events into the basis for a truly memorable (and extended) date together. The same could be arranged for couples who would like to see the Nationals for such diversified activities as ice skating, gymnastics, dance, chess, bridge, and (yes) log-rolling.

Lovers who prefer the outdoors might consider any of several high-adventure experiences, such as whitewater rafting, a trek in the Sierras, or a mountain-climbing expedition to an accessible peak—or a simple camping trip that involves just a little hiking; bike-riding in the countryside; or (heaven forbid!) just relaxing.

As was said earlier, it takes just a little more effort to turn a regular date into a romantic date extraordinaire. You can make *any* date—swifty, an overnighter, a week-end, or a trip-length deal—a memorable event when you are armed ahead of time with some romantic ideas and, when necessary, up-to-date brochures.

Romantic Vacations

There is nothing more fulfilling to a true romantic than to spend time alone with his or her loved one—a *lot* of time. Vacations are the perfect way to do this, especially if they are well-thought-out, novel, and interesting. The following are four prime "love tour" suggestions.

Alaska

Have you ever wanted to visit (or even explore) Alaska? Tauck Tours (203-226-6911) offers a thirteen-day experience that includes breakfast at the famous Space Needle Restaurant in Seattle, gold-mining at the Little Eldorado Gold Camp in Fairbanks, a ride on the sternwheel riverboat *Discovery*, a visit to Mount McKinley, a three-hour floatplane trip over some of the most spectacular scenery in North America, visits to Anchorage and Juneau, and a cruise through Glacier Bay on the way back to Vancouver and Seattle.

Tauck also offers an eight-day cruise that begins in Juneau and courses through what is known as the Inside Passage, the inspiration for

Tchaikovsky's *Swan Lake*. Beauty comes alive as your senses are indulged by such breathtaking sights as Tracy Arm, Frederick Sound, Baranof Island, Sitka, Glacier Bay, and Skagway while you explore some of the world's most awesome glaciers and majestic fjords.

Hawaii

If you prefer a warmer American vacation, Hawaii could be just the ticket. Classic Hawaii Custom Vacations (800-221-3949) can help you create a dream vacation for two at any of over one hundred properties on six different islands (Hawaii, Kauai, Lanai, Maui, Molokai, and Oahu). They will help you design your own itinerary, arrange for all your needs while in Hawaii (including air and ground transportation and golf packages), and suggest some experiences you might not want to miss. For example, you could trek along on a Hawaiian Safari, go scuba diving around the famous Atlantic Reef, cruise with the crew of the *Atlantis* submarine, fly the Hawaiian sky via a helitour of any number of exotic locales, hook into sportfishing, and even a ride in a 1935 Waco biplane. With a little preplanning, Hawaii can truly become paradise rediscovered!

Club Med

Your choice of a vacation spot that has an even more exotic island flavor can be had through the very popular Club Med (800-258-2633). The Club offers escapes for couples to such romantic places as French Polynesia, the Caribbean, and the Bahamas, giving them the opportunity to leave "real life" behind and fall in love all over again. Its resort villages on Columbus Isle (Bahamas), Paradise Island (Bahamas), Turkoise (Turks and Caicos), Caravelle (Guadeloupe), Buccaneer's Creek (Martinique), Cancún (Mexico), Playa Blanca (Mexico), Sonora Bay (Mexico), Moorea (French Polynesia) and Bora Bora (French Polynesia) are havens designed for romance.

At a Club Med, couples can spend their days relaxing alone or can choose from a wonderful list of his-and-hers activities, including swimming, scuba diving, water ski-

ing, sailing, wind surfing, snorkeling, golf, and tennis. And for those who love an active nightlife, Club Med offers evening entertainments and nightclubs!

Club Med also offers romantic cruises in the Caribbean, the Mediterranean, Southeast Asia, and the South Pacific, all aboard custom-designed ships that will lend the same top-quality "feel" to your experience that you will always enjoy at any of its resorts.

Europe

A vacation in Europe, as arranged by Cosmos Tourama (800-888-7292), offers some of the best values available. Cosmos manages over fifty tours ranging in length from eight days to thirty-two days, depending on where you and your loved one would like to go and what you would like to do. The pace is yours, based on the tour you choose.

Destinations on Cosmos tours include some of the most romantic cities in Austria, Belgium, Denmark, Egypt, England, Finland, France, Germany, Greece, Holland, Hungary, Ireland, Israel, Italy, Liechtenstein, Luxembourg, Monaco, Morocco, Norway, Poland, Portugal, Russia, Scotland, Slovakia, Spain, Sweden, Switzerland, Turkey, and the Balkan countries. Imagine seeing Venice at night from a gondola, sipping champagne in Paris, visiting a casino in Monaco, or swimming off the French Riviera, as you listen to modern Romance languages being spoken around you!

Of course, if you would like to see Europe on your own and at your *own* pace, there *is* an alternative to rigidly scheduled tours: Der Tours (708-692-6300).

Der Tours lets you take advantage of travel by rail. Train travel in Europe is safe, comfortable, and fun; you can luxuriously go to all the places you want to visit while enjoying the scenery and arrive at to your destination relaxed and refreshed. This wonderful means of transportation makes it possible for couples to plan a romantic European vacation that includes as many as seventeen countries (depending on your desires) while you travel on a Eurailpass and stay in some of the nicest accommodations available all along the way. In many ways, this is the ultimate in romantic vacations, allowing you to explore Europe—and each other—at your own leisure.

Other possibilities abound. To take that first step, just call your travel agent. That will be one step the both of you will remember for a long, long time.

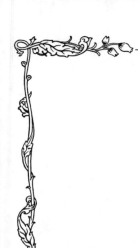

Exotic Vacations

Have you ever imagined what it would be like to spend a vacation on a practically deserted island in the South Pacific? Or to be flown to some of the world's most exotic cities in a "private" jet? Or to travel Europe or the Far East on the Orient Express? Or to take a month-long transatlantic cruise in accommodations fit for royalty? If you have, your dreams can at last come true!

Turtle Island

Set in the unspoiled Yasawa Islands of exotic Fiji, Turtle Island is the 500-acre private island that was used to film both the original and the remade versions of the movie *The Blue Lagoon*.

Chosen as Island Resort of the Year in 1988, as one of the world's Ten Most Romantic Hideaway Resorts in 1991, and as a perennial *Lifestyles of the Rich and Famous* Top Ten Resort, Turtle Island is a place of wonder and discovery. The resort limits the number of guests to just fourteen couples (after all, there are only fourteen private beaches available), who spend their time luxuriating in the beauty of this wondrous Pacific island and sharing experiences with their loved one that will remain with them the rest of their lives.

Gourmet picnics on a private island or a private beach, horseback riding along the island trails, deep-sea fishing (yellowfin tuna, dorado, sailfish, marlin, and wahoo are just some of the game fish you might catch), snorkeling, sailing, exploring the underwater wonders in a glassbottom boat, scuba diving among virgin reefs, and swimming and windsurfing in the famous Blue Lagoon are just some of the activities that you as guests can enjoy. You can also visit a nearby Fijian village, experiencing the natives' way of life while sharing a drink with the village chief.

Turtle Island also offers a Fijian sunset wedding ceremony to couples wishing either to get married or to renew their wedding vows. The bride is brought to her husband-to-be (both are dressed in custom-made, traditional Fijian wedding attire) on a beautifully decorated raft rowed by two Fijian men as the groom awaits her on a white sand beach. Her arrival is announced by the trumpeting of conch shells and the beating of drums. As the couple are led to the outdoor altar, they are greeted by a Fijian choir singing in the background. After the ceremony (Catholic or Protestant clergy are available to perform any wedding), the newlyweds (or "reweds") are carried on a throne to a wedding feast in their honor that features roast pig, seafood, and other local delicacies. Then comes the traditional wedding cake. It is an experience that no couple will ever forget. And the marriages are perfectly legal.

Guests stay in private *bures* (seaside bungalows) along the Blue Lagoon. Each has a bedroom with a queen-size, four-poster bed, a private sitting room fully stocked with some of the finest wines in the world (as well as French champagnes and tropical juices), two full bathrooms, and vaulted ceilings.

As the evening approaches, cocktails and dinner are announced by musicians strolling among the bungalows, serenading guests with the music of lali drums and guitars. Meals served at a long communal table (with the other guests) comprise such exotic fare as freshly caught lobsters, crabs, oysters, local fish, and a variety of other culinary delights harvested from the sea—as well as some of the finest beef dinners in the world (from Australia). The romance of the meals, however, is not limited to the menu. It is also in the locale, and in the after-dinner entertainment by the talented Figian staff.

Dinners usually are served in a range of sites that include a mountaintop with a spectacular panoramic view and the beach looking out on the splendor that is the

South Pacific. However, couples who desire more quiet moments together can request a private gourmet dinner set in a romantic and remote location on the island.

The true beauty of Turtle Island is the gifts you leave it with—a renewed dedication to your relationship, shared experiences that you will treasure forever, lifelong friendships formed with the other guests and the caring staff, and the discovery that indeed life _can_ be a truly beautiful experience.

To request a video (and any other information) about this wonderful vacation spot, call Turtle Holidays at 800-826-3083 or 206-256-4347.

The Private Jet

For some of you who prefer a little more adventure in your life, a tour by "private" jet might be the answer to your dream vacation. And TRAVCOA (Travel Corporation of America) is the answer.

You are picked up by a chauffeured limousine and taken to your hometown airport, where you are flown first-class to your "private" jet. There you will be greeted by experienced tour guides and fourteen carefully selected cabin attendants whose sole concern is your comfort.

Once aboard your "private" jet (an L-1011 which has been reconfigured from a 360 passenger plane to luxury transportation for forty-eight couples), you begin a trip of wonder and romance complete with stays in some of the most luxurious hotels in the world, unforgettable gourmet dining experiences for two, and special entertainment in some of the most exotic cities in the world. This truly is romance at its finest!

A recent thirty-day group tour left from Los Angeles and had layovers in Sydney (Australia), Hong Kong, and Singapore—from which it traveled by the famed Eastern and Oriental Express to Penang (Malaysia) and Bangkok (Thailand). Once again boarding their "private" jet, they continued on to Muscat (Oman), Cape Town (South Africa), and Nairobi (Kenya)—where they experienced the thrill of a safari, and a hot-air balloon ride affording a beautiful view of African wildlife. They then flew to Istanbul (Turkey), and on to Malaga (Spain), where a privately chartered cruise ship took them to Gibraltar, Rabat (Morocco), Casablanca, and Tenerife (Canary Islands). There they

boarded their "private" jet for the last time and flew to New York, where they bid new-found friends farewell and were returned home via first-class air passage and chauf-feured limousine, having completed the adventure of a lifetime.

For more information on upcoming "private" jet tours, call TRAVCO at 800-992-2003.

The Orient Express

If you believe that the essence of romance is a combination of intimacy, ambience, and mystery, then a trip on the Orient Express (as envisioned by Maupintour Gold Tours) might be the answer to your dream vacation. And if you love Europe, their European Treasures package is one you simply don't want to miss!

Gold's seventeen-day package trip takes you to Rome, where you will marvel for three days while taking in the sights and sounds of that wondrous, historic capital built on a hill. From there a bus carries you in comfort to Florence (the city that nurtured such creative geniuses as Leonardo da Vinci, Michelangelo, Dante, and Galileo), where you will enjoy two nights before moving on to its final destination, Venice, the most romantic of *all* cities. While there, you and your loved one will be served dinner in a private villa that overlooks the Grand Canal, and be encouraged to create memories of your own.

After two wonderful nights in Venice, you and your loved one board a private cabin on the Venice Simplon—Orient—Express, for a leisurely rail ride to Paris while taking in the sights of the European countryside and enjoying the finest French cuisine as well as the most luxurious rail travel.

During your four-night stay in the City of Light, you and your loved one will be shown through the incredible Palace of Versailles and the vineyards of the Champagne region, and toast your good fortune on a private dinner cruise.

The final leg of your trip is again aboard the Venice Simplon—Orient—Express, which takes you to London, where you will experience your choice of London theatrical performances, as well as a visit to the Palace of Westminster, and a private lunch at the Victoria and Albert Museum, before flying home from Hzathrow Airport.

This is romance, European style.

If you prefer, you can take the Asian Elegance Tour, which features the Orient Express plus the mysterious attractions of the Far East. This thirteen-day trip begins with a flight from Los Angeles to Hong Kong, where you and your loved one will spend three nights as a guest of one of the world's premier luxury hotels and enjoy the sights and culture of one of the busiest port cities in the world. From Hong Kong, you are flown to Bangkok for four nights in Thailand, where you will enjoy the best of Thai hospitality, a cruise on the *Oriental Queen*, a visit to Chiang Mai ("Rose of the North"), and visits to some of the most beautiful sites you will ever see.

From Bangkok, the Eastern and Orient Express takes you for a luxurious ride through Malaysia in a private cabin. As the train makes its way to Singapore, you and your loved one will enjoy luxurious meals and experience the fascinating cultural panorama that the Far East has to offer.

After two wonderful nights in Singapore, it will be time to return to Los Angeles with truly romantic memories of the days and nights you spent together in the Far East—and aboard the unforgettable Eastern and Orient Express.

For more information on Maupintour Gold tours, call 800-255-4266.

The Transatlantic Cruise

If all of this has seemed—well—hectic, then how about a luxurious thirty-day cruise that begins in wonderful, wonderful Copenhagen (Denmark) and ends in the Big Apple (where else)? The Silversea Grand TransAtlantic package could be just the one for you!

After being flown to Copenhagen, you and your loved one are escorted to a luxury suite aboard your cruise ship, *The Silvercloud*, on which you will be treated like royalty. Ports of call will include Lubeck (Germany), Tallinn (Estonia), St. Petersburg (Russia), Helsinki (Finland), Stockholm (Sweden), Ronne (Denmark), Zeebrugge (Belgium), London (England), Hull (England), Leith (Scotland), Inverness (Scotland), Kirkwall (Orkney Islands), Stornoway (New Hebrides), Douglas (Isle of Man), Holyhead (Wales), Dublin (Ireland), Waterford (Ireland), and Cork (Ireland) before continuing on to seven relaxing days at sea and your arrival at New York City.

Guests onboard are treated as just that—guests, *not* mere passengers. Renowned

chefs from all over the world offer unique delicacies that are created with flair and presented for your enjoyment at your table set for two.

When you are not enjoying a little quiet time alone in your suite, eating gourmet meal selections, or visiting one or another of the exotic ports of call, you and your loved one will have an enormous number of daytime activities available to you on your floating island. Swimming, snorkeling, water skiing, and windsurfing are just a few of the "outdoor" sports available onboard. Or you can stay in shape by visiting the extensive Spa and Fitness Center. If, on the other hand, you prefer indoor activities, there are (for example) chess and bridge competitions, a library, guest speakers, and a Panorama Lounge that offers you spectacular view of the ocean as the two of you are serenaded by piano music. Everything is for your enjoyment.

At night, you can choose to be entertained by fantastic productions in the Show Lounge, dance until the early hours of the morning, stroll in the moonlight on the deck, try your luck in the casino, or simply stay in your suite enjoying popcorn, a private movie—and each other.

All you need to do in order to make reservations for this romantic trip for two is call 800-722-6655.

You and your loved one will cherish romantic adventures for the rest of your lives, enjoying your memories of them all the more because of the efforts you put into making each dream of them a reality!

The Ultimate Gift

The ultimate gift that you can give your loved one is not a cruise around the world, a fancy car, his or her dream house, or even an expensive piece of jewelery. It is *yourself*!

While this may sound simplistic, check it out by asking yourself how much time you spend working, sleeping, and doing other things that don't involve your loved one. Also, ask how much of the time you *do* spend with your loved one is *quality* time—in other words, time spent doing things together, not on watching TV or doing things around the house, on the computer, and so on. Finally, ask how much of this rather small part of your life is spent pursuing new experiences that help you two grow together and remind you both (both consciously and subconsciously) of what attracted you to each other to begin with. The answer should bother you.

Although a span of sixty to eighty years doesn't count for much on the evolutionary scale, it *is* a long time to *us*. The nicest part of this gift of longevity that we have been given is that we have been provided with the means to be happy throughout its duration. Besides furnishing us with our most human qualities (our language, and our abilities to reason and to develop cultures), the human brain makes it possible for us to be aware of, and plan for, the needs of others as well as ourselves, and to joyfully

use this knowledge to bring happiness to those around us. Especially to the ones we love most.

Learning to Be Happy

Giving of yourself is not as easy as it sounds. It takes commitment. To begin with, you need to start to think of your life here as being a heavenly experience. After all, heaven is the place where dreams come true. It is a wonderful place, full of opportunities and the freedom to be happy. It is a mythical world filled with terrific people, endless opportunities to contribute to others, the privilege of self-determination and the independence to be anyone and do anything we want to. It is a universe where love is everything and careers are simply a means to create security for that love, not replace it. It is heaven on earth.

People who are truly happy understand this. They appreciate the special gift we have all been given, even though their personal definition of happiness may be different from someone else's. They laugh a lot, knowing that laughter is therapeutic, a tension-reliever. Besides, it is impossible to be depressed when you are laughing. Laughter releases endorphins into your brain that gives it a sense of well-being, a natural high.

Happy people view life as a series of opportunities rather than a succession of problems. They know that no one has to be a victim and that the key to being happy is to take responsibility for their own happiness. They derive contentment, fulfillment, and joy from living. They constantly use sad events and news to reevaluate the way they look at the world and to gain a better understanding of who they are and how they will savor the world they live in. Their inner needs are satified by, as Nietzsche put it, "taming our demons and turning them into divine children." In fact, they believe in themselves and the future and make conscious decisions that affect their actions and reactions, leading to predictable situations with positive outcomes. They trust themselves to act and react in a self-aware manner. In short, happy people do not simply exist, they truly *live*, marching through life consciously, with genuine purpose and high self-esteem.

By learning to be happy and have a positive outlook on life, you will have taken the next step in giving of yourself to your loved one. You will be fun to be around and will begin to see life for the wonderful experience it truly is!

"Be happy while y'er leevin,
For y'er a lang time deid."
—ANONYMOUS SCOTTISH
MOTTO FOR A HOUSE

Self-Awareness

The next step in giving of yourself is to learn to be honest with yourself. Take a look at your life and evaluate how difficult it really is, as opposed to how difficult you have made it for yourself. If a problem exists with your loved one (or in any other part of your life), determine how much of the problem *you* really are and what you can do to improve the situation. Decide what kind of life you would like to share with your loved one, evaluate what your life together has become, and be aware of the excuses you give yourself regarding why it cannot be different. *Everything* is possible!

People who are in love and truly happy don't take themselves or their troubles too seriously. They see situations that arise in their lives as opportunities, not problems, and have fun solving them—together. They feel fulfilled!

Openness

Awaken the trust that you had in yourself as a child. Redevelop that long-lost innocence and wholeness that gave you independence from your surroundings and a sense of control over your destiny. Learn to take control of the wonders of your brain, and use it to bring you joy.

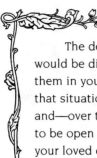

The decision to *want* to be more open is not the same thing as *being* more open. It would be difficult to *be* trusting and open before you make a conscious decision to *want* them in your life. But once you make that decision, the first thing you will notice is that situations you once viewed as problems are no longer as overwhelming as before, and—over time—will actually become opportunities. Eventually your decision to want to be open and trusting will result in a much happier and satisfying relationship with your loved one!

"Love is blind; friendship closes its eyes."
—ANONYMOUS FRENCH QUOTATION

Goals

The next step is to set goals for your own life and your life together. Having made the decision to be happy and open, you need to determine what your personal priorities really are (not what you have been told they should be) and take a step toward making them a reality. This is where self-honesty and openness pay off. By looking deep within, you derive a lot of insight into who you are and what brings you the most satisfaction, excitement, and fulfillment. By translating these priorities into goals, you end up taking the first substantial step toward giving yourself to your loved one.

How successful you are in this step depends on your commitment to succeeding. Listing the advantages and benefits you will derive from achieving goals you have chosen for your life, and the life you will share with your loved one, would be a powerful motivator. The comfort zone we all have in our lives is a very powerful self-defeater, since it views any change in behavior as a threat and reacts accordingly. You have to *want* to change and *believe in* the reasons and benefits of the change.

The opportunity we encounter as we take this step is that we are not simply changing a specific area of our life. We are actually affecting our whole approach to it. The decisions we made in the past were *life* decisions. Once made, they affected us for a very, very long time.

This step creates a whole new set of life decisions—each a positive change that will result in happiness (if you have been honest with yourself). Each with a wonderful payoff that will bring you and your loved one happiness for years to come.

By listing and accepting the positive advantages to making this new set of life decisions, you give yourself the strength to overcome the adversity created by your comfort zone.

Self-Acceptance

Achieving your personal goals becomes much easier if you learn to accept yourself for what you are—a human being capable of greatness, yet susceptible to making mistakes. As human beings, we have the unique ability to learn from our mistakes. It is one of our greatest talents. Anyone who operates under the unrealistic expectation of constant perfection or places unreasonable demands upon themselves cannot be happy. These expectations destroy self-esteem and, together, are the most effective self-defeating mechanism that our comfort zone has in its arsenal in its efforts to prevent us from reaching our new goals. To a perfectionist, sufficiency or adequacy is tantamount to failure. To someone who judges self-worth according to unrealistic demands, it is never "What have I done?" but rather "What have I done *recently*?"

The same thing applies to people who allow themselves to be treated as doormats or who must have absolute control over every aspect of their lives or who exist by rebelling against everything society stands for. They accepted unhappiness through a self-motivated unconscious decision made years earlier, in childhood, that foreordained future failure.

The interesting thing about this is that it is easy to spot *someone else* overdoing it or expecting too much. It is very clear when *someone else* allows abuse, or is a control freak. And we avoid the individual who is always rebelling against something, bringing disharmony and negativism into the lives of those around them. But somehow we seem to miss it when *we* are guilty of that sin.

This anticipation of failure (if you expect to be perfect all the time or to achieve the impossible over and over again, then you *will* fail because you set yourself up to

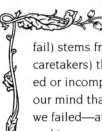

fail) stems from our childhood. At a young age we found out (i.e., were told by our caretakers) that we were either overachievers or underachievers, smart or dumb, talented or incompetent. Once we believed this, we set up a one-person judge and jury in our mind that judged our performance from then on. We had an *expectation* of failure. So we failed—at least in our own mind and in the unforgiving eyes of our internal judge and jury.

By learning to accept ourselves for what we truly are (not what we have been told we are), we set out on the road to high self-esteem and are able to pursue our goals effectively. If we cannot accept ourselves as wonderful human beings, how can we ask or expect our loved ones to?

Loving Habits

Once you have gained self-acceptance, you are well on your way to achieving self-love and high self-esteem—provided you are willing to work on developing good habits. Habits that will make you successful in both your personal life and your love life.

Happy people, as was said earlier, are proactive: They make things happen; they don't wait for them to happen. They have clear-cut goals for their life and that of their loved one; they work at finding creative ways to make them a reality and break up the journey to the fulfillment of those goals into small, loving, enjoyable steps; and they prioritize their time (so they don't waste any valuable time that could be spent with their loved one). Happy people listen with both their ears and their hearts, are always cognizant of being fair, take the time to understand the needs of both their loved one and those around them, and constantly seek to improve themselves by expanding their horizons, developing their minds, and challenging their abilities. Finally, they *find time* for themselves (time to look within and renew a wonderful acquaintance) *and* their loved one. Time for introspection and rest. Time to rejuvenate the mind, the body, and the soul. Time to constantly rekindle the flame of love! And they "practice, practice, practice" and "reevaluate, reevaluate, reevaluate"—every chance they get.

Take the time to ask yourself how you are doing. Redefine your definition of happiness. Revise your goals. Reexamine your habits. Revitalize your plan for your life together. It is only through constant growth that love (and life) do not stagnate.

Every successful journey begins with a small first step. After that, each step gets easier and easier. Once you take the first small step necessary to give of yourself to your loved one, you will discover that you have embarked on a journey of wonder, discovery, and joy. Your life together will become richer and fuller and will have more meaning. You will in truth have given your loved one the "ultimate gift."

"I crown thee king of intimate delights,
Fire-side enjoyments, home-born happiness."
—WILLIAM COWPER

Romantic Marriage Proposals

 true romantic quite literally lives and breathes romance. No matter what the situation, he or she finds creative, loving ways to make it better. Proposing marriage is a perfect example. Once you have decided that you want to spend the rest of your life with your loved one, start the journey with the right first step—a truly romantic marriage proposal. One your lover will cherish and talk about for the rest of your lives together!

Romantic marriage proposals are best made in intimate situations—although there are always exceptions to the rule. One true romantic took her soon-to-be-fiancé to a ball game and had an airplane skywrite above it his name plus "I love you. Will you marry me?" and then "Love," followed by her name. The whole crowd shared their joy.

Another romantic asked his loved one's favorite entertainer to propose on his behalf at a concert they attended together. She loved it! And other romantics have been known to propose marriage via messages lit up on the side of the Goodyear blimp, on billboards, and by announcing their intentions in a public place.

For the record, however, grand gestures are not always the most romantic way to propose, and can easily backfire. Your loved one may not want to be embarrassed or put on the spot in the slightest. In fact, a mar-

riage proposal is best made in an intimate setting where you can most fully and genuinely relish your joy and cherish the moment that will bring your two lives together in a special way. It does not need to be expensive or grandiose—just from the heart, and romantic.

If you are thinking about proposing marriage, consider one of the following ideas—or use them to inspire an idea of your own:

♥ Take your loved one on a picnic where you will be surrounded by beauty. It might be by a river or the ocean where you can take a romantic walk, by a lake or pond where you can go for a romantic boat ride (canoe or rowboat), on a mountain or at the top of a skyscraper where you can share a panoramic view of the beautiful world we live in, or any other spot you both find romantic. In the early evening, sharing a beautiful sunset is especially romantic.

♥ A nice touch might be to hide the engagement ring (if a guy can give one to his girl, why can't a girl give one to her guy?) in a Cracker Jack box or at the bottom of a champagne (or other favorite beverage) glass. You might even inscribe the ring with "I will love you always! [your name]." When your lover finds it, say, "This ring is as genuine as the love I feel for you. Will you marry me?"

♥ Another way to propose marriage would be to prepare a romantic candlelight dinner for your partner and present her or him with a very special handwrought scroll containing the marriage proposal when you serve dessert, asking your intended to read it. A suggestion for its title might be "I Promise You"—and it could read something like this:

I promise to always be faithful and loving.
I promise to always work at making you happy.
I promise to make every day a new loving experience for you.
I promise to always be there for you.
I promise to always be sensitive to your needs and desires.
I promise to always remember special days dear to both of us.
I promise to always love and accept you as you are.
I promise to always try to give you the moon and the stars.

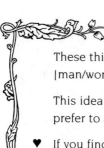

These things I promise to do if you will marry me and make me the luckiest |man/woman| alive today. I love you!

This idea would also work at a nice restaurant that you both find romantic, if you prefer to go out instead of dining at home.

♥ If you find the scroll idea a little too formal, there is a more humorous variation you can try. Have your favorite florist deliver to the restaurant a bouquet of flowers and helium-filled "Love" balloons that has a note attached which reads "I love you! Will you marry me?" Just as you are getting ready for dessert, have your waiter deliver it to your table.

♥ Another romantic marriage proposal might come in the form of a drive in the country. Pick a night when you will be able to see the stars clearly, and set out just before sunset. As you watch the sun go down and the stars appear, share your mutual dreams and aspirations, setting the stage for your proposal. Once the stars are out, "notice" how close to the two of you they are, and mention that you can almost touch them. Then reach out as if to grab one, and suddenly pretend that you were successful. Present that "star" to your loved one, saying, "You know, it looks just like an engagement ring. Will you marry me and brighten up my life forever?"

♥ A romantic variation of this might be to go for a ride in the country on a cold or rainy day and develop "car trouble" just as you come to little cottage in the middle of nowhere. A cottage that you have rented just for this purpose—without letting your loved one know. Knock on the door, and when there is no answer, say, "I've got to get help!" and try to open it without even mentioning a key. (With the owner's connivance, you'll succeed.) In spite of any cautions from your mate, go inside—to find a warm fireplace, blankets, some hors d'oeuvres, and champagne waiting. Surprise (and calm down) your loved one by telling her or him that you arranged this for just the two of you—and present your marriage proposal over a glass of the champagne.

♥ Or you might plan a trip to the beach and arrange for your loved one to "find" a beached bottle with a note in it. The note might say, "Help me! My heart is hopelessly lost, and only your love can save me. Will you marry me?"

♥ You might also consider proposing during a trip you take together. If you and your loved one love to ski, there is little more romantic than being alone together in front of a fireplace in a mountain cabin surrounded by snow. (If you prefer warmer climates, you might take a short cruise together and propose as you share the stars and the ocean one evening.)

As long as you are both in love, the right ingredients will always be there to make your marriage proposal magical. Adding a little ambience just makes it that much more memorable!

*Now that you have decided to propose marriage to your loved one,
you should review the following preproposal check list:*

♥ *I'm on a first-name basis with my loved one.*

♥ *I'm not already married.*

♥ *I'm positive that I want to be married and live happily ever after
with my loved one.*

♥ *I'm relatively certain that my loved one and I feel the same way
about each other.*

♥ *I'm ready with my heart medication so the thing won't leap out of
my body when my loved one says yes.*

♥ *I'm prepared to celebrate our newfound life together.*

*If you are satisfied that you can answer yes to all of the statements
that apply to you, go forward, young (or old) lover. The world and all
its beauty await you!*

Wedding Omens and Customs

If you haven't already married your loved one, or at least made plans to be married, then take heed: The following omens have been proven to forecast weddings and happy marriages for generations. Maybe—just maybe—you might be able to ignore them, but that's doubtful. You are probably doomed if you don't pay attention. But that really isn't so bad, is it? After all, what's the point of being a true romantic if you don't have a loving partner to be romantic with?

You (or someone you know) will be married soon *when*:

♥ A chicken enters your house with a straw in its mouth, which it leaves.

♥ A mockingbird flies over your house.

♥ A white dove comes near your house.

♥ A spider descends from the ceiling and "dances" (i.e., goes up and down)

♥ A cow moos during the night

Of course, once you know that you're going to be married, you will find it prudent to take the steps necessary to make certain that your life together will be full of love, joy, and prosperity. So it is with great pleasure that _The Complete Guide to Everything Romantic_ shares the following omens and customs that will ensure your marital bliss.

Your marriage will be a happy one _if_:

♥ You feed a cat out of one of your old shoes just before you are married.

♥ A cat sneezes in front of your bride (or you, if you are the bride) on the day before your wedding.

♥ Either of you dreams about your wedding day.

♥ You marry in June, since "Married in the month of June, life will be one honeymoon" (authorship anonymous).

♥ Your wedding ceremony lasts between half an hour and an hour (the rising hand of the clock denotes rising fortune!).

♥ You are married in the afternoon.

♥ You are married on a beautiful day (rainy weather supposedly forecasts a stormy marriage).

♥ A ray of sunshine falls on you as you leave the church.

♥ It snows on the day of your wedding (snow represents prosperity and happiness).

♥ You see a lamb or a dove on the way to the church.

♥ A flock of white birds flies directly over you on your way to the wedding ceremony.

♥ You carry bread in your pocket and throw it away (representing you throwing away your troubles) or give it to someone who is hungry (forecasting good fortune during your marriage, because of your generosity) on your wedding day.

♥ A spider is found crawling on the bride's wedding dress before the two of you are married.

♥ The bride wears earrings during the marriage ceremony.

- ♥ The bride has her hair done, and her veil put on, by a happily married woman just before the wedding.

- ♥ A new dime is put in the bride's left shoe just before she walks down the aisle.

- ♥ Orange blossoms are used in your wedding decorations (they bring good fortune, since—according the ancient custom—they represent innocence, purity, lasting love, and fertility).

- ♥ You carry a pinch of salt to the church (it will chase away evil spirits).

- ♥ The bridesgroom carries a horseshoe in his pocket during the wedding (a miniature horseshoe will do).

- ♥ The bride cries on her wedding day (it means she has cried all her tears away).

- ♥ You both step into, and leave, the church with your right foot first.

Of course, it isn't enough to know what to *do*. You also need to know what *not* to do. *Don't*:

- ♥ Get married to someone born in the same month as you.

- ♥ Get married on your birthday.

- ♥ Get married during Lent.

- ♥ Postpone your wedding (old customs believed that one of you would die shortly if you did this).

- ♥ Let the bridegroom see the bride in her bridal dress before your wedding ceremony.

- ♥ Let the bride wear pearls on your wedding day (each pearl supposedly represents a tear she will shed during the marriage).

- ♥ Get married in a church with bats (if one flies over you during the ceremony, it will bring you both bad luck).

    Finally, don't believe everything you read!

The key to a successful marriage is—and always will be—how much you love, care about, and listen to each other.

Marry when the year is new,
Always loving, kind and true.
When February birds do mate,
You may wed, not dread the fate.
If you wed when March winds blow,
Joy and sorrow both you'll know.
Marry in April when you can,
Joy for maiden and for man.
Marry in the month of May,
You will surely rue the day.
Marry when June roses blow,
Over land and sea you'll go.
Those who in July do wed,
Must labor always for their bread.
Whoever wed in August be
Many a change are sure to see.
Marry in September's shrine,
Your living will be rich and fine.
If in October you will marry,
Love will come, but riches tarry.
If you wed in bleak November,
Only joy will come, remember.
When December's snows fall fast,
Marry and true love will last.

—Anonymous

Wedding Vows

The marriage ceremony is a brief sacred event that swiftly but profoundly changes the remainder of two people's lives for as long as they remain a wedded couple—and often well past that point. Its intangible but demonstrable power to bond and bind both the bodies and souls of its principal participants is perhaps its greatest blessing.

Marriage rites have been around for about as long as civilization itself, and are as varied as they are plentiful. They range from the commonly used words from "The Celebration and Blessing of a Marriage" in *The Book of Common Prayer* ("Dearly beloved: We have come together in the presence of God to witness and bless the joining together of this man and this woman in Holy Matrimony...") to personally written vows. The alternatives are seemingly endless, offering a rich set of choices for any couple looking to make their wedding day (or the day they reaffirm their original vows) special.

The next several pages show some of the more popular secular and non-secular marriage-ceremony materials used today.

Put on therefore, as the elect of God, holy and beloved, bowels of mercies, kindness, humbleness of mind, meekness, long-suffering;

Forbearing one another, and forgiving one another, if any man have a quarrel against any: even as Christ forgave you, so also do ye.

And above all these things put on charity, which is the bond of perfectness.

And let the peace of God rule in your hearts, to the which also ye are called in one body; and be ye thankful.

Let the word of Christ dwell in you richly in all wisdom; teaching and admonishing one another in psalms and hymns and spiritual songs, singing with grace in your hearts to the Lord.

And whatsoever ye do in word or deed, do in the name of the Lord Jesus, giving thanks to God and the Father by him.

—Colossians 3:12-17, *Holy Bible*, King James Version

Have you not read that he who made them from the beginning made them male and female, And said, For this cause shall a man leave father and mother, and shall cleave to his wife: and they twain shall be one flesh? Wherefore they are no more twain, but one flesh. What therefore God hath joined together, let not man put asunder.

—Matthew 19:4-6, *Holy Bible*, King James Version

Thus saith the Lord: Again there shall be heard in this place... The voice of joy, and the voice of gladness, the voice of the bridegroom, and the voice of the bride, the voice of them that shall say, "Praise the Lord of hosts: for the Lord is good; for his mercy endureth forever..."

—Jeremiah 33:10-11, *Holy Bible*, King James Version

Be thou magnified, O bridegroom, like Abraham, and blessed like Isaac, and increase like Jacob, walking in peace and living in righteousness...

And thou, O bride, be magnified like Sarah, and rejoice like Rebecca, and increase like Rachel, being glad in thy husband and keeping the bounds of the law..."

—from the Greek Orthodox marriage service

We thank thee, O Lord God almighty, who art before the ages, master of the universe, who didst adorn the heavens by thy word, and didst lay the foundations of the earth and all that is therein; who didst gather together those things which were separate unto union, and didst make the twain one. Now again, our Master, we beseech thee, may thy servants be worthy of the mark of thy Word through the bond of betrothal, their love for one another inviolable through the firm sureness of their union. Build them, O Lord, upon the foundation of thy holy Church, that they may walk in accordance with the bond of the word which they have vowed one to another; for thou art the bond of their love, and the ordainer of the law of their union. Thou who hast brought about the oneness, by the union of the twain by thy words, complete, O Lord, the ordinance of thine only-begotten Son Jesus Christ our Lord, through whom and together with all-Holy Spirit be praise to thee now and always.

　　—from the Coptic Orthodox marriage service

Therefore must the bride below have a canopy, all beautiful with decorations prepared for her, in order to honor the Bride above, who comes to be present and participate in the joy of the bride below. For this reason it is necessary that the canopy be as beautiful as possible, and that the Supernal Bride be invited to come and share in the joy.

　　—from "Terumah," in *The Zohar*

My beloved spake, and said unto me, Rise up, my love, my fair one, and come away. For, low, the winter is past, the rain is over and gone;

The flowers appear on the earth; the time of the singing of birds is come, and the voice of the turtle is heard in our land;

The fig tree putteth forth her green figs, and the vines with the tender grape give a good smell. Arise, my love, my fair one, and come away.

　　—Song of Solomon 2: 10-13, *Holy Bible*, King James Version

Set me as a seal upon thine heart, as a seal upon thine arm: for love is strong as death; jealousy is cruel as the grave: the coals thereof are coals of fire, which hath a most vehement flame.

Many waters cannot quench love, neither can the floods drown it: if a man would give all the substance of his home for love, it would be utterly contemned.

—Song of Solomon 8: 6-7, _Holy Bible_, King James Version

You Abound in Blessings, Adonai our God, who creates the fruit of the vine.
You Abound in Blessings, Adonai our God,
You created all things for Your Glory.
You Abound in Blessings, Adonai our God,
You created humanity.
You Abound in Blessings, Adonai our God,
You made humankind in Your image, after Your likeness, and You prepared from us a perpetual relationship. You Abound in Blessings, Adonai our God, You created humanity.

May she who was barren rejoice when her children are united in her midst in joy. You Abound in Blessings, Adonai our God, who makes Zion rejoice with her children.

You make these beloved companions greatly rejoice even as You rejoiced in Your creation in the Garden of Eden as of old. You Abound in Blessings, Adonai our God, who makes the bridegroom and bride to rejoice.

You Abound in Blessings, Adonai our God, who created joy and gladness, bridegroom and bride, mirth and exultation, pleasure and delight, love, fellowship, peace and friendship. Soon may there be heard in the cities of Judah and in the streets of Jerusalem, the voice of joy and gladness, the voice of the bridegroom and the voice of the bride, the jubilant voice of bridegrooms from their canopies and of youths from their feasts of song. You abound in blessings,

Adonai our God, you make the bridegroom rejoice with the bride.

—The Hebrew "Seven Blessings" (Sheva Berahot)

We have taken the seven steps. You have become mine forever. Yes, we have become partners. I have become yours. Hereafter, I cannot live without you. Do not live without me. Let us share the joys. We are word and meaning, united. You are thought and I am sound.

May the nights be honey-sweet for us; may the mornings be honey-sweet for us; may the earth be honey-sweet for us; may the heavens be honey-sweet for us.

May the plants be honey-sweet for us; may the sun be all honey for us; may the cows yield us honey-sweet milk!

As the heavens are stable, as the earth is stable, as the mountains are stable, as the whole universe is stable, so may our union be permanently settled.

—from the Hindu marriage ritual of "Seven Steps"

O Lord Fire, First Created Being! Be thou the over-lord and give food and drink to this household. O Lord Fire, who reigns in richness and vitality over all the worlds, come take your proper seat in this home! Accept the offerings made here, protect the one who makes them, be our protector on this day, O you who see into the hearts of all created beings!

—Hindu wedding prayer

Nothing happens without a cause. The union of this man and woman has not come about accidentally but is the foreordained result of many past lives. This tie can therefore not be broken or dissolved.

In the future, happy occasions will come as surely as the morning. Difficult times will come as surely as night. When things go joyously, meditate according to the Buddhist tradition. When things go badly, meditate. Meditation in the manner of the Compassionate Buddha will guide your life.

To say the words "love and compassion" is easy. But to accept that love and compassion are built upon patience and perseverance is not easy. Your marriage will be firm and lasting if you remember this.

—Buddhist marital homily

When our two souls stand up erect & strong,
Face to face, silent, drawing nigh & nigher,
Until the lengthening wings break into fire
At either curved point...what bitter wrong,
Can the earth do us, that we should not long
Be here contented? Think, ...in mounting higher,
The angels would press on us, and aspire
To drop some golden orb of perfect song
Into our deep, dear silence. Let us stay
    Rather on earth, Beloved!—...where the unfit
Contrarious moods of men recoil away
    And isolate pure spirits, and permit
A place to stand & love in, for a day,
    with darkness and the deathour rounding it.

—ELIZABETH BARRETT BROWNING,
FROM SONNET XXIII
Sonnets From the Portuguese

Let me not to the marriage of true minds
Admit impediments; love is not love
Which alters when it alteration finds,
Or bends with the remover to remove.
O, no; it is an ever-fixed mark

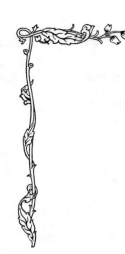

That looks on tempests and is never shaken;
It is the star to every wand'ring bark,
Whose worth's unknown, although his highth be taken.
Love's not Time's fool, though rosy lips and cheeks
Within his bending sickle's compass come
Love alters not with his brief hours and weeks,
But bears it out even to the edge of doom.
    If this be error, and upon me proved,
    I never writ, nor no man ever loved.

—WILLIAM SHAKESPEARE, SONNET 116

Love one another, but make not a bond of love:
Let it rather be a moving sea between the shores of your souls.
Fill each other's cup but drink not from one cup.
Give one another of your bread but eat not from the same loaf.
Sing and dance together and be joyous, but let each one of you be alone,
Even as the strings of a lute are alone, though they quiver with the same music.
Give your hearts, but not into each other's keeping.
For only the hand of life can contain your hearts.
And stand together yet not too near together:
For the pillars of the temple stand apart
And the Oak tree and the Cypress grow not in each other's shadow.

—KAHLIL GIBRAN, *The Prophet*

The Marriage Ring

The ring, so worn as you behold,
So thin, so pale, is yet of gold:
The passion such it was to prove—
Worn with life's care, love yet was love.

—George Crabbe

The modern custom of giving engagement and then wedding rings became popular in the days of the Roman Empire, when betrothal rings were given as tokens of love. Initially, these rings were made of iron, since only people in positions of authority could wear rings made of gold. However, as Rome became more powerful in its influence and more affluent, other Roman citizens were allowed to use gold until, over time, all betrothal rings came to be made of gold. Marriage rings became popular in the fifth century and eventually were recognized by the church. Today, both rings are given as a celebration of two people's love for each other and their commitment to each other.

Tertullian (ca. 155 –220 A.D.), a great writer for the early church and a leading advocate of gold betrothal rings, wrote about gold: "[Being] the nobler and purer metal and remaining longer uncorrupted, [it] was thought to intimate the generous, sincere, and durable affection which ought to be between the married parties."

Romantic Honeymoons

ost couples think of a honeymoon as being for newlyweds only. In fact, honeymoons are for repeaters and recon-firmers of marriage as well—a celebration of new commitment or a testament to the years of joy shared as well as of the passion yet to come.

A honeymoon, unlike even the best "still single" romantic vacation, is more of a "two's company, three's a crowd" type of holiday than anything else. Couples spend their time enjoying their special relationship, concentrating on the love they feel for each other, rather than looking for activities that distract them from each other. Simply put, honeymoons are the most romantic of all vacations, whether two people are first starting life as a married couple or reaffirming their love with a second, third, or twenty-fifth celebration of their nuptials.

A great many resorts and hotels offer honeymoon packages, including all the companies and resorts mentioned in the chapters titled "Romantic Vacations" and "Exotic Vacations." Honeymoons can range from the very exclusive (including the one with the marriage ceremony on Turtle Island mentioned in "Exotic Vacations") to a less grand but very satisfying one quite close to home. Your travel agent can be of great assistance in helping you to select one that fits your budget nicely.

The three companies that offer the widest selection of affordable yet exotic honeymoon packages are Club Med (see "Romantic Vacations"), ATS Tours (800-

423-2880), and Islands in the Sun (800-828-6877).

Both ATS Tours and Islands in the Sun have the distinction of catering to couples planning a second (or later) honeymoon, as well as to first-timers. Four of their more popular packages include the Australia Honeymoon, the Bora Bora Honeymoon Deluxe, the Fiji Honeymoon, and the Tahiti Honeymoon Deluxe.

♥ The Australia Honeymoon Package (ATS Tours) is an eleven-day, eight-night affair just for couples who want to experience the Land Down Under. It features round-trip airfare to Australia from Los Angeles via Air New Zealand; four nights on Hamilton Island (including an excursion to the Great Barrier Reef, a Premier Room at Hamilton Towers, and dinner at the Outrigger Restaurant); four nights in Sydney (including a Harbor View Room at the Renaissance Hotel, and a cruise of the harbor); and special gifts for the honeymooners.

♥ The Bora Bora Honeymoon Deluxe Package (Islands in the Sun) is an eight-day sojourn. It features round-trip airfare from Los Angeles to Tahiti via Air France; two nights at the Tahiti Beachcomber Parkroyal in an Overwater bungalow; five nights at the Bora Bora Lagoon Resort; breakfast brought to you in an outrigger canoe; and a host of special gifts and touches that honeymooners really appreciate.

♥ The Fiji Honeymoon Package (ATS Tours) is a twelve-day, nine-night stay in paradise. It features round-trip airfare from Los Angeles to Fiji via Air New Zealand; five nights at the Yasawa Island Lodge in one of eight private, secluded, one-bedroom villas known as _bures_; four nights at the Regent of Fiji in a Deluxe Garden Room; and assorted gifts as only the Fijians can give to those in love. It is a truly relaxing way to fall even deeper in love!

♥ The Tahiti Honeymoon Deluxe Package (Islands in the Sun) offers honeymooners round-trip airfare from Los Angeles to Tahiti via Air New Zealand; two nights at the Tahiti Beachcomber Parkroyal, two nights at the Moorea Beachcomber Parkroyal, and three nights at the Bora Bora Moana Beach Parkroyal—all in Overwater bungalows; a dinner cruise on the Bora Bora Lagoon; and a lot more.

The one thing that great honeymoon packagers have in common is an under-

standing that a honeymoon is for two people who want to be pampered in an unob-
strusive way as they enjoy spending time alone. Whether you plan a honeymoon in the
South Pacific or the Poconos or in your own backyard, remember that you already have
the *primary* ingredients needed to make it a success—each other!

The word honeymoon *didn't become part of our vocabulary until
the sixteenth century. Prior to that, the practice was referred to as*
going away *by people of a genteel upbringing, and* honey-month
*by everyone else. The original custom dates back to the days when a
groom often "captured" his bride, and so had to stay away from his
new father-in-law until that gentleman calmed down. The couple usually stayed out of the way for at least a month—just in case!*

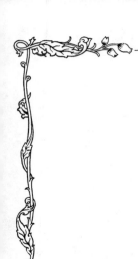

Parting Notes

f you were to ask me to summarize in just two words what the main ingredient to romance is, I would say "caring imagination." Simply put, without imagination there can be no long-term romance—and without romance, few prospects for long-term love.

As a parting thought, I offer a little story, originally from Amenophis II (ca. 3300 b.c.), about a man whose imagination concerning romance is still with us five thousand years later:

Long ago, in ancient Egypt, a pharaoh fell in love with a beautiful princess. Because of her youth, the princess's father refused consent to their marriage. The pharaoh, being a wise man, desired to have the father's blessing and so agreed to wait until the princess was of age. His love for her grew daily, and he longed for some way to show his devotion to her while he was waiting for their marriage.

The pharaoh called in the royal jewelers and told them to search the land for the most precious stone in existence. This the pharaoh had mounted on a ring of gold and took it to his loved one. As he slipped the ring on her finger, he told her, "Until I can place a wedding band on your finger and claim you for my bride, wear this ring as a reminder of my devotion. Just as the gem is priceless, so is my love for you!"

Down through the ages, the engagement ring has served as a pledge of true love, and as a symbol to the rest of the world that two people have chosen to spend their lives together.

Caring imagination.